Developing effective school management

It is increasingly being recognised within the profession that those taking on the management of curricular or pastoral teams need specific training in the skills of management in order to tackle the complex responsibilities of the middle management role. However, this is an area in which there has tended to be a training gap. In this book, Jack Dunham makes a significant contribution towards redressing the balance and helps teachers to identify and develop the knowledge and skills needed to become effective middle managers in primary or secondary schools. He focuses on four main areas: staff management, management skills, professional development and change, and stress management. This book will be invaluable to all those seeking or already acting in the crucial middle management role in schools.

Jack Dunham is a freelance management and stress management consultant in education and industry, and is also a tutor at the School of Education, University of Bristol. He has worked as a teacher, educational psychologist and training officer. His publications include *Stress in Teaching* (Routledge 1992).

Educational Management Series

Series editor: Cyril Poster

Developing effective school management

Jack Dunham

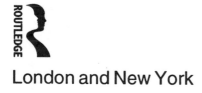

London and New York

First published 1995
by Routledge
11 New Fetter Lane, London EC4P 4EE

Simultaneously published in the USA and Canada
by Routledge
29 West 35th Street, New York, NY 10001

© 1995 Jack Dunham

Typeset in Palatino by LaserScript, Mitcham, Surrey
Printed and bound in Great Britain by
Biddles Ltd, Guildford and King's Lynn

British Library Cataloguing in Publication Data
A catalogue record for this book is available from the British Library

Library of Congress Cataloging in Publication Data
Dunham, Jack
  Developing effective school management/Jack Dunham.
  p. cm. – (Educational management series)
  Includes bibliographical references and index.
  1. School management and organization. I. Title. II. Series.
  LB2805.D88 1994
  371.2 – dc20   94-18584
                                                                          CIP
ISBN 0–415–10428–9 (hbk)
ISBN 0–415–10429–7 (pbk)

Contents

Figures

Tables

Training materials

Foreword

Jack Dunham's book *Stress in Teaching*, the second edition of which was published by Routledge in 1993, demonstrates the high quality of his appreciation of the needs of teachers. This new book draws on a wealth of experience in training and consultancy for middle managers, both in schools and industry. Middle managers feel, quite rightly, that their school tasks and responsibilities have increased at the very time when the time to discharge them has decreased. This book offers much that will make the use of that limited time more effective.

This is not a book looking 'from the outside in'. The author frequently quotes the views of teachers on his workshops on the problems that they have met with that have inhibited their ability to do the job as they see it; and as often he provides the varied responses of groups within the workshop to the management training tasks they have been set. This is therefore a book of potential practical benefit to middle managers and aspirants to promotional posts.

Cyril Poster

Introduction

This very practical guide is written for teachers holding curricular or pastoral management posts in secondary or primary schools and for teachers who want to prepare themselves for these posts. It will also help those who want to increase their effectiveness and job satisfaction by developing their skills at managing time pressures, curricular and organisational changes, teamwork and stress.

The guide contains much of the information, teamwork exercises, self-awareness checklists and practical exercises used in my management courses for teachers in the Further Professional Studies Unit in the School of Education, University of Bristol, and in different primary and secondary schools. A number of these activities are also used in my work as a management consultant in industry. These exercises and activities enable course members to learn to use the key management skills which are required for effective human resource management. These requirements are identified by myself and the members at the beginning of each course as the objectives we seek to achieve by the end of the course. This method has also been used in this book. Most of the chapters begin with a short list of objectives which provide a framework for learning to develop the essential management skills. Teachers on my courses provide most of the examples of management behaviour and situations which are analysed, discussed and sometimes strongly criticised during the course work. These examples do not always illustrate good management practice. They are included in this book so that readers can also analyse, discuss and develop a critical awareness of how these situations might be handled differently.

It is good for me to have the opportunity to acknowledge the contributions of teachers and managers in industry to my courses, to this book and to my learning in the ten years since I became an educational and industrial consultant. They are committed, caring and enthusiastic, in spite of working in circumstances which are the most turbulent and disruptive they have ever experienced.

My learning has also been enriched by the contributions of my wife

Vivien, who is a deputy head in a secondary school. My editor, Cyril Poster, has helped me to improve my writing skills and has shown much patience in our coaching sessions. My secretary, Jane Curtis, and her husband, Dale, have shown a high level of persistence in unravelling my script and my editor's comments to meet the deadlines.

I am grateful to all these contributors and pleased to present the results of our combined efforts for the reader's attention.

Chapter 1

The importance of whole school management

THE URGENT NEED FOR MIDDLE MANAGEMENT TRAINING

The need for greater involvement in school management of those in middle management posts has been strongly recommended in a School Teachers' Review Body Report. It argues that 'substantial improvements' are needed in several aspects of school management (School Teachers' Review Body 1993: 6). It is particularly critical of those heads, deputies and senior teachers who are:

- failing to focus on pupil achievement;
- making policy decisions but failing to implement them;
- failing to make full use of those in middle management positions;
- showing themselves to be concerned with efficient administration at the expense of 'good strategic management';
- failing to motivate or set clear targets.

The report sensibly identifies some barriers to good practice in school management (ibid.). It is critical of a number of factors, which include:

- the lack of support available to senior management teams because of the dwindling role of local education authorities and the sharp reduction in their advisory services;
- the lack of 'shorter more practically oriented courses' for management training;
- the large number of curricular and organisational reforms being introduced into schools without the improvements in management skills which are needed to implement them effectively;
- the mainly administrative role which too many deputy heads have in too many schools which caused the Review Body to conclude: 'This is not a cost-effective use of a relatively expensive resource' (TES 1993: 6). The teachers in one secondary school put their conclusion more directly during a staff meeting to discuss the school's budget: 'Why don't we get rid of a deputy?'
- the low level of non-contact time for primary teachers. In my experience,

this is a very important factor in the constraints on those teachers with co-ordinators' responsibilities, which have been greatly increased by the demands of the National Curriculum.

These problems identified by the School Teachers' Review Body seem to indicate that the changes required by the Education Reform Act of 1988, which have been introduced in rapid succession since then, cannot be carried out effectively without substantial improvements in management policies and practices, and a much more widespread use and appreciation of management skills. This means a whole school model of management, in which members of staff, both teaching and non-teaching, governors, parents and pupils are all actively involved in all relevant activities concerned with the effective use and development of the school's re-sources, such as people, buildings, equipment, money, space and time.

THE PROBLEMS CAUSED BY MANAGERS' LACK OF TRAINING

The need for the improvement of management skills throughout the school can also be expressed from a perspective rather different to that of the School Teachers' Review Body. This alternative viewpoint is con-cerned with the implications for teachers of the problems caused by poor management and the problems experienced by managers. Of particular concern are the great demands made on those members of staff holding middle management positions, demands which may be unrecognised by colleagues because of their lack of experience of leading a team, chairing a meeting, motivating a member of the team to meet a deadline and all the other aspects of middle managers' roles.

Problems caused by poor management can be recognised in the fol-lowing three reports from experienced teachers on my Bristol University courses. The first is from a secondary head of year:

It is part of the government's stated aim to reveal those schools whose attendance figures are poor. Truancy is a problem for many schools and each school has no doubt devised its own strategies for recording the figures and dealing with the problem. However, in order to publish figures which are meaningful in any way, it is necessary to standardise the way in which registers are kept. The proposal in my school was to create three categories: presence, authorised absence and unauthorised absence. Whilst this may seem to have simplified the system, there were two main problems that arose. First was the fact that the cate-gories did not fully define what counted as authorised or unauthorised absence, and secondly the new system was to be introduced half-way through a term when the old system had been used up until that time.

In my school, registers are taken by tutors under a house system led by five heads of house. The new system was passed to the heads of

house by the deputy head of administration with no further instructions. The result was confusion. Tutors did not know what counted as
an authorised absence and when they asked the heads of house for
guidance, they did not know either. Decisions obviously needed to be
made quickly, but the deputy head of administration was reluctant to
make decisions without reference to the LEA which wanted to wait
until a meeting was convened. Moreover, because there had been no
instructions as to when the new system was to be introduced, the
various heads of house introduced it at different points. Some introduced it immediately, others waited until the half term break and
others still were wanting to wait until the end of the term. Tutors in
some houses were aware that other tutors were not implementing the
new system and were thus annoyed that they were having to do it and
suffer the confusion.

The consequence was twofold. First of all, at the end of the year, by
which time the process had been agreed by all those involved, the
figures obtained were not standardised even within the school, let
alone between other schools. The purpose for which the new system
had been introduced had therefore not been met. This consequence
was foreseen as inevitable at an early stage and merely aggravated the
resentment felt by those who had to implement it during the year. The
second consequence was stress. This was caused by confusion where
tutors did not know what they were supposed to be doing or if they
were doing it right. There was frustration at having to undertake an
administrative task whose objective they knew would not be met, and
there was anger and resentment at the haphazard way the new system
had been introduced with little or no explanation.

A similar situation arose with a circular form from the LEA which
required various structures to be observed by schools when reporting
to parents on the child's progress. This circular arrived within two
months of the end of the summer term and required that schools
should include on the child's report information that would enable
parents to compare their child's performance to that of other children.
This was to be done by publishing figures of results and attendance for
all children in the same year and was to be effective from July 1st.

In order to do this properly, not only would teachers of several
subjects have had to re-test pupils across the year, but reports which
had already been written would have to be scrapped and new forms
printed which would allow for the recording of such information. This
would have involved an enormous amount of extra work and additional
expense at a time when teachers were desperately trying to organise
themselves for the new syllabuses which were to become operational the
following term. Fortunately, common sense prevailed and the schools
met together with the LEA and agreed a new date for introduction.

It is therefore clear that whilst government or local authority policy can introduce pressures, incorrect or insensitive implementation of those policies can increase these pressures to unnecessarily stressful levels. Clearly, a structured introduction of new policy is needed that recognises and takes into consideration the demands made upon the workforce. Time is obviously one important factor and being given too short a notice to do things leads to stress. Combined with this and equally significant is the time when a new policy is to be implemented. Certain policies can, no doubt, be introduced in the middle of a school year, but others need to come in at the start. Another important factor is clarity. Had the tutors known and understood the new system of registration before it was introduced then confusion would not have arisen. If instead of being passed straight down the line, senior management had examined what was involved and possibly consulted with the middle managers, many of the problems met could have been avoided.

The fact that the LEA was receptive to the change in the reporting system suggests that it might have been receptive to similar complaints about the registration changes. A major difference between these two was the fact that senior management had to implement the former whilst it was essentially middle managers and the workforce that had to operate the latter. This is not to suggest that the senior management only looks after itself, but it does indicate a lack of sensitivity on the part of senior managers to the pressures on the workforce and an unawareness of the stress that can result.

The second report is from a secondary head of department:

High stress levels at my school can be attributed to the poor quality of leadership skills displayed by the senior management team; even simple decisions are delayed and major decisions are frequently followed by a change of mind. There are serious problems of communication between staff and senior management. Staff are angry that their opinions are never sought even when their department is directly concerned. Any consultation is seen as purely cosmetic – an exercise in keeping the staff 'involved' even when they are not. The general consensus is that senior management do not care about the staff – their workload or their welfare. Staff feel they are adrift in a ship without a captain.

The latest example of this is the imposition of a timetable without any negotiation or consultation with heads of department, a timetable felt to be unworkable by many staff who are now too apathetic to take action. Only the PE department still have enough energy to fight back, perhaps because they have a weapon to fight with. They have withdrawn their goodwill and refused to organise Sports Day, which had to be cancelled.

The third report is from a secondary PE teacher:

> The need for understanding and communication is vitally important. The role of the middle manager is critical here. Lack of communication can result in unnecessary stress, as was the case recently in our department. Failure by our head of department to communicate properly with the curriculum deputy head led to unnecessary confusion and stress about a member of the department's timetable the following year. As is so often the case in our subject, paperwork is left to the last as the practical nature of the subject is seen as paramount. This inevitably leads to poor communication with the senior management team and the subject is seen therefore as always getting the raw end of the deal with curriculum time. With so much changing in education today it is vital that paperwork is given attention and turned around quickly and efficiently so the best arrangement is negotiated for staff within the department and not left, as in this case, to the last minute.

The teachers on middle management courses have identified several different kinds of problems. Most of their management difficulties appear to be concerned with 'people problems', for which they have had little or no training. Some members of a recent course briefly reported the following difficulties:

- 'One of the teachers in my departmental team has not worked up to our standard for the last six months, but I have not reprimanded him. Now if I start to criticise, I will have to bring up all those complaints. I should have acted much earlier.'
- 'I told one of the deputy heads about one of my department who was not meeting deadlines. The deputy over-reacted and really blasted this person, making my job so much more difficult.'
- 'Two members of my Science department never keep deadlines. The reason is they are moonlighting an evening job. I have tried everything without success. What do I do?'
- 'If a member of my team does not complete something on time I do it for them. It is easier and causes less stress to do it than to complain about it.'

Lack of training has been reported also to be a major cause of some of the worst difficulties experienced by primary school coordinators in their jobs. Wortley (1993) has discussed the experience of teachers on B.Ed. courses who had been appointed to subject coordinators' posts in Northern Ireland. She reports a case study from research carried out by teachers on an in-service Bachelor's degree course. The following report summarises the experience of a primary school coordinator:

> The coordinator had little training for her new responsibilities. 'I was

given a copy of the Cockroft Report and it was suggested I might find something useful in it.' Sensibly the coordinator responded to her colleagues' training needs thus: They were experiencing difficulty with writing schemes of work even if they were expressed by chance remarks such as 'What are we going to do about subtraction?' She arranged for a workshop on 'Teaching Subtraction' though she had no training in leading workshops. The workshop generated further ideas and identified further training needs. She received little guidance and support from her Principal who 'may have been piqued that ordinary teachers were being offered a management role'.

(Wortley 1993: 47)

These problems of lack of training and lack of support for coordinators were also reported in a discussion paper prepared for the Department of Education and Science by Alexander, Rose and Whitehead (1992), known as the 'Three Wise Men', who recommended that headteachers need to spell out thoroughly the responsibilities and the accountabilities for coordinators and provide support to enable them to discharge their executive responsibilities.

How to provide support and training in terms of the knowledge, skills and attitudes which are required by coordinators to fulfil their responsibilities and accountabilities effectively and with personal satisfaction are not specified by Alexander *et al.*, but a suggestion by Wortley could be a helpful starting point: 'A strategy emanating from the primary school chalk face . . . has more prospect of surviving and flourishing' (1993: 47).

The coordinator's strategies of starting from the training needs of her colleagues, and Wortley's suggestion of basing strategies for training and support on the recommendations of teachers, provide excellent guidance for this book.

IDENTIFYING TRAINING NEEDS

My strong belief is that to help those having middle managers' roles to improve their management skills, and those aspiring to these posts to develop these skills and become effective much more quickly when promoted, it is good practice to ask them what help is needed. The teachers start my management courses by discussing in sub-groups of three or four what they want to achieve during the course. The whole course consists of about 16 teachers who have been appointed or are seeking appointment to middle management posts. To this group each sub-group now makes a presentation of their objectives. Their presentation may take many different forms and the following examples from recent courses (Figures 1.1, 1.2, 1.3, 1.4 and 1.5) show the wide range of training needs identified.

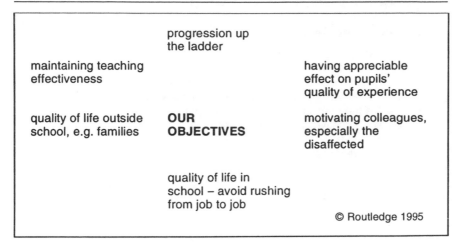

progression up
the ladder

maintaining teaching
effectiveness

having appreciable
effect on pupils'
quality of experience

quality of life outside
school, e.g. families

**OUR
OBJECTIVES**

motivating colleagues,
especially the
disaffected

quality of life in
school – avoid rushing
from job to job

© Routledge 1995

Figure 1.1 Presentation of objectives (1)

Our objectives are:

- recognition and development of personal skills
- to become more aware of a wider range of management styles than already experienced
- preparation for career advancement
- learning to avoid the pitfalls of poor management
- learning to get the most from colleagues
- to listen

© Routledge 1995

Figure 1.2 Presentation of objectives (2)

Promotion stakes:

- how to show an interest in developing the position we hold
- how to make the necessary effort to develop self
- how to apply general management principles to the teaching situation
- as a head of department, to find best way of organising time/duties/resources of permanent and peripatetic staff (in the light of having to buy in to the peripatetic music service – perhaps!)
- meet with other people to exchange ideas (especially because of isolation in private sector) in the present climate of CHANGE

© Routledge 1995

Our objectives are to:

- acquire management skills
- gain from each other's experience
- gain greater self-confidence in meetings
- remain sane when taking on increasing responsibilities
- explore the question: Is middle management for me?
- develop effective time management
- sell ourselves: acquire techniques
- find out what managers do!
- find out what the differences are between pastoral/academic management
- learn how to get the best out of the people we might manage
- learn about financial management
- learn how to keep up and assimilate new initiatives
- balance school life against social life: when to stop working
- remain effective in the classroom with extra pressures
- develop confidence in our professional abilities
- discover our limits
- improve our present role
- strengthen our self-esteem
- learn assertiveness skills

© Routledge 1995

Figure 1.4 Presentation of objectives (4)

We want the course for:

interview techniques	developing support techniques
taking stock	management styles
personal assessment	team building
direction	cooperation
time management	improving performance
boosting confidence	stress management

© Routledge 1995

Figure 1.5 Presentation of objectives (5)

ACHIEVING COURSE OBJECTIVES

The courses seek to help members achieve their objectives by the course-work discussions and activities, and by the preparatory reading which is required before each week's session. An equally important focus for learning to develop the skills which will satisfy training needs is the past and current experience of members in their schools. Members are advised to follow a recommendation that a bridge between school and a university course is established by following these guidelines:

- Discuss the course programme and your objectives for taking this course with a member of the senior management team.
- Arrange regular interviews with this person to discuss the university work and bring comments from her/him to the first sessions.
- Ask if s/he will discuss her/his role in school with you.

The invitation to course members to identify their management training objectives, and the recommendation that they should achieve them by 'making bridges' between course work and school experience under the guidance of a school colleague, acting as a mentor, are just as relevant and important for readers of this book. Each chapter starts with a statement of objectives, and guidance towards achieving them is given. However, readers are encouraged to substitute or add their own objectives and to use past and present experience to augment the learning strategies recommended in each chapter.

IDENTIFYING LEARNING STYLES AND MANAGEMENT SKILLS

A valuable framework for enhancing our opportunities to learn from experience has been provided by Honey and Mumford (1986: 15). They believe that a learning experience is only fully effective when the main stages in the learning processes have been planned and followed. This converts a learning opportunity into a learning experience.

These stages are given in Figure 1.6.

Stage 1
Having an experience

Stage 4   *Stage 2*
Planning the next steps   Reviewing the experience

Stage 3
Drawing conclusions from
the experience

© Routledge 1995

Figure 1.6 Learning from the 'experience circle'

This may not be as straightforward as it sounds. Readers may not be equally effective in all the stages of the learning circle because of differences in their learning styles. Honey and Mumford have identified four main styles as Activist, Reflector, Theorist and Pragmatist, which correspond to the four stages of the learning circle. They have developed a questionnaire to enable people to gain more information about their preferences for these four styles. To enable readers to become more aware of their preferences, they should complete the learning styles questionnaire, marking the schedule and profile indicator (Honey and Mumford 1989: 19).

The Honey and Mumford learning styles questionnaire

This questionnaire is designed to find out your preferred learning style(s). Over the years you have probably developed learning 'habits' that help you benefit more from some experiences than from others. Since you are probably unaware of this, this questionnaire will help you pin point your learning preferences so that you are in a better position to select learning experiences that suit your styles.

There is no time limit to this questionnaire. It will probably take you 10-15 minutes. The accuracy of the results depends on how honest you can be. There are no right or wrong answers. If you agree more than you disagree with a statement, put a tick by it [✓]. If you disagree more than you agree put a cross by it [✗]. Be sure to mark each item with either a tick or a cross.

1 I often take reasonable risks if I feel they are justified.   [ ]
2 I tend to solve problems using a step-by-step approach, avoiding any 'flights of fancy'.   [ ]
3 I have a reputation for having a no-nonsense, 'call a spade a spade', style.   [ ]
4 I often find that actions based on feelings are as sound as those based on careful thought and analysis.   [ ]
5 The key factor to judging a proposed idea or solution is whether it works in practice or not.   [ ]
6 When I hear about a new idea or approach I immediately start working out how to apply it in practice as soon as possible.   [ ]
7 I like to follow a self-disciplined approach, establish clear routines and logical thinking patterns.   [ ]
8 I take pride in doing a thorough, methodical job.   [ ]
9 I get on best with logical, analytical people and less well with spontaneous, 'irrational' people.   [ ]

10 I take care over the interpretation of data available to me and avoid jumping to conclusions. [ ]

11 I like to reach a decision carefully after weighing up many alternatives. [ ]

12 I'm attracted more to new, unusual ideas than to practical ones. [ ]

13 I dislike situations that I cannot fit into a coherent pattern. [ ]

14 I like to relate my actions to a general principle. [ ]

15 In meetings I have a reputation for going straight to the point no matter what others feel. [ ]

16 I prefer to have as many sources of information as possible – the more data to consider the better. [ ]

17 Flippant people who don't take things seriously enough irritate me. [ ]

18 I prefer to respond to events on a spontaneous, flexible basis. [ ]

19 I dislike very much having to present my conclusions under the time pressure of tight deadlines when I could have spent more time thinking about the problem. [ ]

20 I usually judge other people's ideas principally on their practical merits. [ ]

21 I often get irritated by people who want to rush headlong into things. [ ]

22 The present is much more important than thinking about the past or future. [ ]

23 I think that decisions based on a thorough analysis of all the information are sounder than those based on intuition. [ ]

24 In meetings I enjoy contributing ideas to the group just as they occur to me. [ ]

25 On balance I talk more than I should and ought to develop my listening skills. [ ]

26 In meetings I get very impatient with people who lose sight of the objectives. [ ]

27 I enjoy communicating my ideas and opinions to others. [ ]

28 People in meetings should be realistic, keep to the point and avoid indulging in fancy ideas and speculation. [ ]

29 I like to ponder many alternatives before making up my mind. [ ]

30 Considering the way my colleagues react in meetings I reckon, on the whole, I am more objective and unemotional. [ ]

31 In meetings I'm more likely to keep in the background than to take the lead and do most of the talking. [ ]

32 On balance I prefer to do the listening rather than the talking.   [ ]
33 Most times I believe the end justifies the means.   [ ]
34 Reaching the group's objectives and targets should take precedence over individual feelings and objections.   [ ]
35 I do whatever seems necessary to get the job done.   [ ]
36 I quickly get bored with methodical, detailed work.   [ ]
37 I am keen on exploring the basic assumptions, principles and theories underpinning things and events.   [ ]
38 I like meetings to be run on methodical lines, sticking to laid down agenda.   [ ]
39 I steer clear of subjective or ambiguous topics.   [ ]
40 I enjoy the drama and excitement of a crisis.   [ ]

© Routledge 1995

Training material 1.1   The Honey and Mumford learning styles questionnaire

Scoring the Honey and Mumford questionnaire

Put a tick in the appropriate place corresponding to your answers to the questionnaire and total them.

1 _ 4 _ 12 _ 18 _ 22 _ 24 _ 25 _ 27 _ 36 _ 40 _
Total Activist _

8 _ 10 _ 11 _ 16 _ 19 _ 21 _ 23 _ 29 _ 31 _ 32
Total Reflector _

2 _ 7 _ 9 _ 13 _ 14 _ 17 _ 30 _ 37 _ 38 _ 39 _
Total Theorist _

3 _ 5 _ 6 _ 15 _ 20 _ 26 _ 28 _ 33 _ 34 _ 35 _
Total Pragmatist _

© Routledge 1995

Training material 1.1   The Honey and Mumford learning styles questionnaire (cont'd)

Learning styles preferences

Activist	Reflector	Theorist	Pragmatist	
20	20	20	20	
19				
18		19		
17			19	Very strong preference
16	19	18		
15			18	
14		17		
13	18	16	17	
12	17	15	16	Strong preference
	16			
11	15	14	15	
10	14	13	14	
9	13	12	13	Moderate preference
8				
7	12	11	12	
6	11	10	11	Low preference
5	10	9	10	
4	9	8	9	
3	8	7	8	
	7	6	7	
	6	5	6	
2	5	4	5	Very low preference
	4		4	
1	3	3	3	
	2	2	2	
	1	1	1	
0	0	0	0	

After filling in your score, double the number you scored in each section, circle the appropriate numbers and draw lines to connect.

Training material 1.1 The Honey and Mumford learning styles questionnaire (cont'd)

Honey and Mumford have also provided further details of each of these learning style preferences:

Activist

Strengths

- flexible and open-minded;
- happy to have a go;
- happy to be exposed to new situations;
- optimistic about anything new and therefore unlikely to resist change.

Weaknesses

- tendency to take the immediately obvious action without thinking;
- often takes unnecessary risks;
- tendency to do too much him or herself and hog the limelight;
- rushes into action without sufficient preparation;
- gets bored with implementation/consolidation.

Reflector

Strengths

- careful;
- thorough and methodical;
- thoughtful;
- good at listening to others and assimilating information;
- rarely jumps to conclusions.

Weaknesses

- tendency to hold back from direct participation;
- slow to reach a decision;
- tendency to be too cautious and not take enough risks;
- not assertive.

Theorist

Strengths

- logical thinkers;
- rational and objective;
- good at asking probing questions;
- disciplined approach to thinking.

Weaknesses

- restricted in lateral thinking;
- low tolerance for uncertainty, disorder and ambiguity;
- intolerant of anything subjective or intuitive;
- full of 'shoulds, oughts and musts'.

Pragmatist

Strengths

- keen to test things out in practice;
- practical, down to earth, realistic;
- businesslike – gets straight to the point;
- technique oriented.

Weaknesses

- tendency to reject anything without an obvious application;
- not very interested in theory or basic principles;
- tendency to seize on the first expedient solution to a problem;
- impatient with waffle;
- on balance, task oriented not people oriented.

Honey and Mumford believe that we learn from experience most successfully when our learning styles match the opportunities we have.

Readers can respond positively, therefore, to a wide range of opportunities for learning to develop their management skills by having some of the characteristics of each of the four styles of Activist, Reflector, Theorist and Pragmatist. They can take advantage of every chance which is offered to them or which they make for themselves to use these styles to learn the skills of middle management. These have been identified by the teachers on my courses as decision making, listening, organising, delegating, planning, motivating, team work, evaluating, consulting, defining the task, assertiveness, monitoring, negotiating and the use of effective management styles. These skills, which are not in any order of importance, form the learning opportunities of this book. We make a start with the next chapter, which is concerned with effective management styles.

Chapter 2

Effective management styles

This chapter is concerned with helping readers achieve the following objectives:

- increasing awareness of management styles;
- identifying management styles;
- developing management styles;
- identifying what constitutes acceptable and unacceptable management styles.

INCREASING AWARENESS OF MANAGEMENT STYLES

There are many different ways of using the management skills recommended towards the end of the previous chapter. How they are used is a very important factor in their effectiveness. The need for those in management positions to become more aware of their management styles is shown clearly in the following two reports from middle managers. The first is from a head of department:

When a school is threatened with closure or suffering from falling rolls, and swift action is needed, the authoritarian style is frequently used. My experience, however, suggests that this is not always an appropriate style. If the Head is a trusted, respected, charismatic leader, seen to represent the staff, autocratic control may ensure the school weathers the storm. When my own school faced closure, the Head adopted an extremely directive style. For some time the staff had been growing suspicious of him and he was losing their respect and trust. The situation was exacerbated when he submitted a scheme to the LEA, whereby the school would escape closure by being turned into a sixth form college; his proposals were rejected by both the LEA and his staff, thus hastening his premature retirement. The directive style is also inappropriate when people are at their peak and know exactly what to do, how to do it and are successful; to use this style in these circumstances would decrease motivation, create resentment and possibly lower performance. Furthermore, I personally do not believe a directive style is appropriate for sensitive issues such as appraisal or innovation and would not use it for the coordination or management of teams.

The second report is from a head of year:

> I have not previously attempted to fully take stock of my style or my effectiveness as a leader. I believe that many pupils see me as a rather severe, autocratic leader. This is a role I have been uncomfortable with for some time yet have found difficulty in extricating myself from. The time has come when I need to begin some form of self-review for myself.
>
> As a preliminary to setting up some form of appraisal within my team of year tutors I asked them to assess my style of management. The experienced form tutors felt that I was too autocratic and they wanted more freedom and participation in decision-making. Those staff who are much less experienced as group tutors saw me as being much more democratic. One even pleaded that I become more autocratic as he felt I was allowing him too much freedom which was actually under-mining his confidence. The rest said they were quite happy about the way I did things and most seemed to respect the way I carry out the professional aspect of the job.

The assessment this head of year was using for his team's review of his management style is shown in Figure 2.1 and follows a framework which is recommended to the members of my courses because of its clarity, relevance for school management and the fact that it highlights a variety of very different styles. It has been developed by Oldroyd, Smith and Lee (1984) from a model by Tannenbaum and Schmidt (1973), as part of their very useful staff development workbook. They identify seven different styles of staff management. A manager:

- makes decision and announces it (1);
- makes decision and sells it to staff (2);
- presents ideas to staff and invites questions (3);
- presents tentative decision, subject to change (4);
- presents problem to staff and selects from staff suggestions (5);
- identifies problem, staff make decision (6);
- Leaves staff to identify problem and make decision (7).

ADVANTAGES AND DISADVANTAGES OF THE DIFFERENT STYLES

Members of my courses report their experiences of using some of the styles outlined in the previous section and of observing their advantages,

1   Mark X on the scale where you would put my styles of management (Note: more than one style if necessary):

- makes decision and announces it;
- 'sells' decision;
- presents ideas and invites questions;
- presents tentative decision subject to change;
- presents problem, gets suggestions, makes decision;
- defines problem, asks group to make decision;
- staff identify problem and make decision.

2   Would you like to see a change in my styles of management? Please give reasons:

3   Rate on a scale of 0 (awful) to 5 (excellent), with comments if wished:

My:	Score 0–5	Comment
discipline		
support of pupils		
support of staff		
relationship with staff		
relationship with parents		
communication upwards		
communication downwards		
decision making		
availability		
ability to delegate		
ability to organise		
inducting of staff		

4   What do you think are my particular:

(a) strengths?
(b) weaknesses?

5   Any other comments:

© Routledge 1995

Figure 2.1 Assessment of management styles

disadvantages and effectiveness in different ways. Four of their present-ations, shown in Figures 2.2, 2.3, 2.4 and 2.5, illustrate the use of these styles by the course members themselves and by their colleagues.

The observant and perceptive teacher in Presentation 4 (Figure 2.5) concluded his analysis with a summary of the management styles used in his school and with a recommendation which I support very strongly:

> Managers in my school try whenever possible to operate within the latter half of the continuum, and the decision-making process is usually effective; however, problems can arise when a decision has been made and agreed upon by all and then at the last minute it's changed because someone else has an idea. Each person who intends

---

Some examples of the use of the seven staff management styles

1   Classroom management
    Close school – bad weather
2   Enrichment fund
3   Innovations
4   New report format/changes
5   Voting
6   Working parties   litter
                         uniform
    Open forum   lockers
7   Staff initiative matters raised at staff meetings

Advantages	**Disadvantages**
1 Quick where no grey areas exist. Seen as decisive.	Inflexible. May be unpopular. May be bad leadership.
2 Staff feel they have had some say. May be better for school in long run.	Not true consultation.
3 Staff involvement.	Time-consuming digression.
4 Input of good ideas can be seen. 'Team' decision.	Make management seem indecisive.
5 Everybody able to be involved. Democratic.	Voting could be 'rigged'! Time consuming.
6 Uses staff expertise. Possible in-depth analysis.	Slow process (boring!). May not be good for school in long run (but usually minor problems).
7 Staff initiative could raise spirits.	Undermines management. Could cause low morale.

© Routledge 1995

Figure 2.2 Presentation of the advantages and disadvantages of the seven management styles (1)

What styles do the leaders adopt? All heads of department/year were given a questionnaire based on the seven management styles. The following table shows an analysis of the results.

	Management style						
	1	2	3	4	5	6	7
Heads of department	0	2	4	2	4	2	3
Heads of year	3	1	2	1	4	4	3
Total	3	3	6	3	8	6	6

The following table lists the occasions when each style is used and the benefits to the subordinates of each style:

Style	When used	Benefits to subordinates
1	General administration. Endorsing school policy. Unimportant matters not directly affecting members of the group.	'It saves time of team members'. In time-orientated tasks to keep team members up to date.
2	When some opposition is expected. Control of department stock. When in a better informed position.	When rapid decisions need to be made. Plug advantages to staff.
3	Major and long-term issues. Allows some staff input within controlled framework. Selection and preparation of pupil coursework.	Opinions can be given. Enables subordinates to explore any eventualities.
4	New junior school syllabus. Running of department. Major and long-term issues. To sound out other departments/team members to see if they are thinking along the same lines.	Allows good ideas to be incorporated. 'No one's perfect' – allows incorrect decisions to be amended.
5	In making policy decisions. Use ideas from others to supplement or replace one's own.	'Encouragement of leadership'. 'Democratic decision making'. 'Prompts thought to be critical and aware'.
6	Devising new courses and modules. Allows freedom of choice.	'Involves opinion and personal choice'. 'All consulted on issues and therefore feel useful'. 'To use others' expertise and experience'. 'Cooperation and good atmosphere'. 'Many have more to contribute than they think'.
7	When overworked. Train members of the group. Delegation of work areas.	Allows individuals to develop. Demonstrates potential. To motivate group members.

© Routledge 1995

Figure 2.3 Presentation of the advantages and disadvantages of the seven management styles (2)

I have experience of working in a pastoral year team over the last two years, which has had a change of head of year. The previous head of year was a man of traditional values who in general tended towards styles 1, 2 and 3 with some use of 4. A girl was transferred because of her disruptive behaviour and influence on her peers. The new tutor was informed of the change (his group selected because of the need to equate numbers) and during the following week the decision to move was 'sold' by the head of year quite informally. On reflection this problem was always to be solved by a change of tutor group and so team or individual discussion was unnecessary. The style adopted led to the quick solution of a problem. More recently the new head of year has met similar situations in a different way. A number of demands for change of tutor group including pupil requests were considered by the head of year at a year team meeting. Adopting style 5, he eventually used a team member's suggestion to defer all tutor group moves bar one. By adopting style 5/6 the year head was able to involve proper discussion and use the group to confirm his suggestions. Team involvement with tutorial matters reinforces the responsibility which they possess!

Figure 2.4 Presentation of the advantages and disadvantages of the seven management styles (3)

to rise to a position of authority in the school establishment must become fully qualified. Not qualified in the academic sense, rather that they must become fully acquainted with the variety of management styles available to the manager. The successful manager, the one that can make positive change, is the one that can adopt his or her style to the situation.

CHOOSING WHICH STYLE TO USE

The recommendation in the previous section should be followed up by choosing acceptable role models and observing the different ways they manage different situations and by assessing the effectiveness of the styles used. Whenever the chance occurs, readers should also practise using different styles for different situations, not just responding to them but sometimes anticipating them. This practice can begin immediately! Readers are invited to work through the exercise on choosing management styles. They should then compare their decisions and reasons with the results presented by a group of course members in Table 2.1.

If the comparison of these results with the reader's decisions and reasons shows discrepancies this does not necessarily mean that the reader has made incorrect decisions based on faulty thinking! The group

Style 1: Manager makes decision and announces it

Example: Head only allowing the minibus to be used by PSV drivers.
Effectiveness: Sometimes this is the easiest way to manage; it tends to be less time consuming and prevents any ambiguity when a matter of safety is concerned. However, the lack of consultation doesn't lead to cooperation and it becomes difficult to ask for cooperation at a later stage.

Style 2: Manager makes decision and 'sells' it to staff

Example: Redistribution of salary points when a senior member of staff left.
Effectiveness: Often used when consultation is inappropriate, as in the example above. Staff cannot discuss the allocation of points. The decision was made by the senior management team and sold to the staff at a staff meeting. This left many feeling dissatisfied because they couldn't see why they couldn't have been consulted; things were not really made very clear to them.

Style 3: Manager presents ideas to staff and invites questions

Example: Rarely used in my school, but occasionally when the LEA sends out directives a staff meeting might be called to clarify the situation.
Effectiveness: This style is not liked in my school. It is a 'dishonest' approach because consultation cannot affect the decision, which can very easily lead to dissatisfaction and division between managers and staff.

Style 4: Manager presents tentative decision, subject to change

Example: Negotiation of the 1265 hours and contracts of service where the senior management team put out draft documents which were commented on by staff and adjusted.
Effectiveness: This can be a very good way to reduce time in the decision-making procedure; it is much easier and quicker to adopt and alter a suggestion than ask staff to comment at the outset. It is valuable because staff have something to work from and it involves them; staff learn from each other. Management learns from staff. The word 'draft' or 'consultation document' is used extensively.

Style 5: Manager or staff presents a problem, manager gets suggestions from staff, makes decision

Example: In my establishment both staff and managers identify the problem; for instance, staff identified a problem to do with the attitude of the Sixth Form to working quietly in the library. The headteacher decided to ask staff for ideas and to suggest solutions. This was done through house meetings which everyone attends. The headteacher then selected the best ideas and announced how improvements could be made.

Effectiveness: Both the head and deputy head feel that this is the ideal way to lead staff. They feel that it gets staff involved in the decision making process and that they accept change more readily. They will understand more of the problems involved and this should help them in future years.

Style 6: Manager identifies problem, staff make decision

Example: The head wanted staff to be present at an open evening for new parents together with groups of pupils involved in some activity. Departments were asked to decide levels of manning and attendance.
Effectiveness: In this particular example, many problems were caused in my department because all members wanted to remain at school and take part in only the first hour of a two-hour open evening. My head of department always negotiates problems with us; however, we all felt that if the head wanted us to participate he should be the one to tell us, not our head of department. The situation was 'resolved' by the head of department telling us when we should attend. In the six years that I have known him this is the first time he has had to do that. This is a useful style of management; however, there are very few decisions that staff are allowed to make. If they do accept responsibility if something goes wrong, managers must oversee any decision in order to veto it if necessary.

Style 7: Staff identify problem and make decision

Example: The GRIDS (Guidelines for Review and Internal Development in Schools) approach to identifying problems in the school. All staff are asked to fill in a questionnaire about strengths and weaknesses in all areas of the school. We then form working parties to improve the weakest areas.
Effectiveness: This style of management totally does away with the managers' input into the decision-making process and is therefore unacceptable on all but a few occasions. Even with the GRIDS approach, managers had some input and they did oversee the final decisions. It was rather interesting that 79 staff thought that careers education was a strength of the school. Two did not and thought it to be a weak area. They were both careers staff.

Figure 2.5 Presentation of the advantages and disadvantages of the seven management styles (4)

of course members ended their analysis with an important postscript: 'The team, the size of the school and the circumstances might modify the styles which would be appropriate in these circumstances.' These three factors could well be quite different in readers' schools to those in the group members' schools.

In these situations, which of the seven styles would you employ?

Decision to be made	Appropriate style	Reason for choice
1 Routine admin. task		
2 Implementing curriculum change		
3 Organising a new trip or visit for Year X		
4 Book ordering		
5 The department given a £2000 special grant		
6 Exam to be restructured for Year Y		
7 Developing departmental appraisal policy		
8 Deciding on a new choice of textbook		

© Routledge 1995

Training material 2.2 Choosing management styles

Table 2.1 Reasons for choice of management styles

Decision to be made	Appropriate style	Reason for choice
1 Routine admin. task	1	Efficiency – consultation inappropriate
2 Implementing curriculum change	6	Legal limits, ownership through involvement
3 Organising a new trip or visit for Year 7/8	5/6	Need framework; group ownership, especially if it is extra-curricular
4 Book ordering	6	Financial limits; ownership
5 The department is given a £2,000 special grant	6	Manager wants a say
6 Exam to be restructured for Year 9	6	No reason given
7 Developing an appraisal policy for the department	4/5	Certain things are non-negotiable
8 Deciding on a new base text	6	No reason given

Exercises like this one do provide useful opportunities to learn to relate management style to real-life situations. Opportunities for learning to achieve the objectives set out at the beginning of this chapter – increasing awareness of management styles, acquiring the ability to identify them, developing management styles and learning what constitutes acceptable and unacceptable behaviour – can also be found by using previous experience in different schools and comparing the management styles which the reader encountered there. One of my students used this opportunity very effectively by comparing the management behaviour of two headteachers:

The headteacher of School A manages the school from an autocratic viewpoint. He will make the decisions on the school day, its format and times, and when, for example, the report deadlines are. He then informs the staff of his decisions. Often the three members of the senior management team are consulted on proposals of less importance, but no-one else. I have never seen this headmaster use anything but style 1.

Each department is accountable to the headteacher but he generally allows them to function without interference. However, if there is criticism of the department, from any source, he will often presume 'guilty, until proven otherwise', demanding to know why he has not been kept informed yet at the same time shying away from any personal contact and communication with staff until this situation occurs.

The staff have little respect for the headteacher, they find him inaccessible, insensitive and unapproachable. They are concerned that they are largely ignored, their work not recognised and that they cannot contribute to school decisions. They are also dissatisfied with the structure, which has no incentives or motivators, and are often hindered by routine duties enforced upon them by the headmaster. Despite this the staff have a great intimacy and work well together even if it is a situation of 'us versus them'.

School B is also a comprehensive school, of 1,800 pupils. The headteacher, senior management and middle management work closely together to try and run the school effectively. All staff are regularly consulted about decisions to be made or are asked for their points of view in solving problems, either in time-tabled staff, department or year meetings. This the headteacher sees as important. The minutes of these are collated for him to read and acknowledge. Different members of each department are also included on the panels of a policy development committee, a curriculum working party and a social education committee.

The headteacher is well respected by the staff, and is thought of as a good manager of people and resources. This headteacher can be seen to use all seven of these styles, usually preferring to use styles 3, 4, 5 and 6, although when called upon will use style 1. He has a strong, caring and friendly personality. Staff feel they can talk to him and in return he is very supportive, for example, helping them to further their professional development by informing them of courses he feels will be of use or interest to them.

INFLUENCES ON THE DEVELOPMENT OF MANAGEMENT STYLES

The student quoted in the previous section was also interested in the reasons for the considerable differences in the management styles of the two headteachers. She considered a wide range of possible explanations:

There are many influences on both headteachers' choices of management styles. Each is accountable to both internal and external sources, parents, governors, LEA, staff and pupils. His pressures could be increased by the media, parental and staff expectations, redevelopment, the introduction of the National Curriculum and LMS, role conflict or from his personal life. His own personality, interests, values and perceptions including his self-perception would give him a bias towards particular styles in dealing with problems.

The headteacher of School B has a range of management styles that seem to be closely related to this management course in its consultative approach. He has attended at least one course that I know of and has done several management courses for headteachers. The ideas presented to him have been taken and put to use in his school. The support of staff is, as I have said, very important to him and I can now recognise what he is trying to do and the way he is doing it. He comes across as sincere. The 'style', whichever style that may be at the time, suits his personality. He is an outgoing and friendly person and this comes across to his staff. His background has made him aware of how to present himself and at the same time fulfil his own wishes and objectives. With staff he prefers to use styles 3, 4, 5 and 6, but within the working parties the style is number 7.

The headteacher of School A is a very status-conscious person. He feels that it is a headteacher's responsibility to make the decisions. These decisions he maintains are always right and when queried has been known to justify his decisions by saying that 'God has told me this is the correct decision'. He therefore manages in an authoritarian way, but his personality is such that he cannot do this well because managing to him is to 'tell' and 'shout', never to encourage. Obstacles seem constantly to be set in his way by staff unhappy with this.

His choice of style could be stress-related, the shouting a form of anger and resentment towards his situation which is directed towards his staff, or maybe it could be a result of being predisposed to this one approach over another because of being frequently exposed to a particular style in the past. I feel this head has a complex personality whose viewpoint on how to manage his staff has never changed, except maybe to become more dictatorial. There seems to be a fear there that to consult is a sign of weakness and criticism of him, and the school can never be constructive only harmful, something to be guarded against.

A student on another course also became interested in the development of different styles of management. She asked staff in senior and middle management posts in her school 'to evaluate by the use of percentage figures the influences on their styles of management'. The factors she suggested were parents, general education, PGCE course, social peer group, political beliefs, religious beliefs, colleagues, your middle and senior management, management training courses and other. She presented the results of her small-scale, school-based investigation in the form of a histogram, shown in Figure 2.6.

The results indicate the importance of role models in the development of management styles: our teachers when we were pupils and students, and our headteachers, deputies and professional colleagues during our careers.

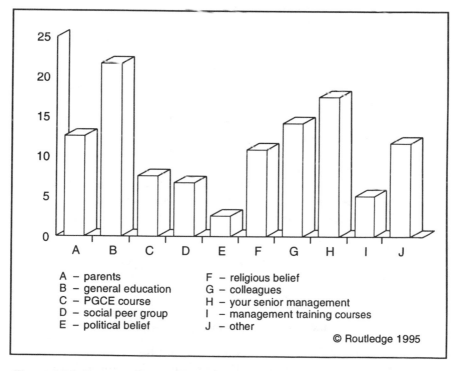

A – parents
B – general education
C – PGCE course
D – social peer group
E – political belief
F – religious belief
G – colleagues
H – your senior management
I – management training courses
J – other

© Routledge 1995

Figure 2.6 Influences on management styles

LEARNING TO DEVELOP A WIDER RANGE OF STYLES

This development suggests to me that the range of styles used by these models may have been quite restricted. Teachers observing and learning from them may have only a small range of styles to choose from in response to situations requiring management decisions and actions in school. It is important for teachers having management posts, and those wanting to have them, to extend their range of available styles to meet situations which are unexpected and perhaps quite out of the experience of the people who were their role models.

In this chapter a number of different methods of learning to develop additional management styles have been discussed. There is one more method I want to use to end this chapter. This approach uses simulated situations, and this example is concerned with a young teacher, Ellie Crowther, having considerable difficulties in her work.

Ellie Crowther is a young, well-qualified teacher who joined the English department with a good reference from her previous school. For the first few weeks of term all seemed to be going well, but in the past month or so staff have become increasingly concerned at reports and evidence of her inability to control her classes. Her attitude in the staffroom is also a worry. She appears to have no friends and is obviously very unhappy, even close to breakdown. The deputy head decides to intervene.

Realising that asking to observe a lesson may disturb Ellie even further, the deputy head 'drops in' on a lesson five minutes after it has started or, to be more accurate, should have started. The presence of a senior member of staff quietens the din and the lesson begins. The content is poor, and the class is profoundly uninterested and uninspired. The organisation of the work is perfunctory. The state of the classroom is appalling: untidy, the work done with her predecessor still on display, but now dusty and covered with graffiti; from a large cupboard dirty PE kit overflows on to the floor. The deputy head observes that the pupils' textbooks are battered, their writing books defaced, untidy and unmarked.

After the lesson the deputy head talks to Ellie. She admits that she has lost interest in teaching since she came to the school. She had enjoyed her first two years of teaching in another county, but now thinks she is not cut out for teaching. The deputy head investigates further over the next few days and finds that:

- Ellie is following the scheme of work, but her head of department has not discussed it with her since the first week of term, being too engrossed with GCSE preparations.

- She has not been required, so she says, to hand in lesson preparation notes to anyone.
- The deputy head is the first person to have seen her teach since she came.
- She teaches in three different rooms in the course of a week, and the class that the deputy head saw is taught in all three, and is very adept at 'forgetting' which one it is meant to be in.
- The room in which she was seen teaching is used by five other members of staff during the week, and the PE Department uses it five times for the 'walking wounded' and stores lost PE kit in the cupboard as there is insufficient storage in the gym.
- Two of her classes are regarded even by experienced teachers as 'not to be wished on your worst enemy on a Friday afternoon'. She has both on a Friday afternoon.

The head decides that some action is called for. Where lies the responsibility for this state of affairs? Who shall see Ellie? Is she the only one to be seen? If not, by whom should any others be seen?

© Routledge 1995

Training material 2.3 Ellie Crowther

The experienced teachers on my courses have proposed a wide range of short-term and long-term strategies for middle and senior management to use to help Ellie find out the reasons for the mismanagement of her work and prevent similar experiences happening to other members of staff in the future. The recommendations of two groups on one course are given in Figures 2.7 and 2.8.

The recommendations are concerned with two kinds of management strategy: personal and organisational. Both are required to achieve the objectives of:

- helping the person with the problem to become effective again;
- planning and implementing the organisational changes needed to prevent a repetition of the situation.

These recommendations also show quite clearly the amount of expertise which becomes available when the human resources in an organisation are tapped. A similar strategy used in industry and in some schools has managers and staff meeting together in small groups to form 'quality circles' (Robson 1984), to make recommendations to solve and prevent many different kinds of problems affecting individuals, departments and the whole company or school.

1   Aims

- remotivate Ellie
- review roles of staff involved

2   Data

- Ellie's opinion
- head of department's opinion
- room allocation
- timetabling
- storage problems
- scheduling of workload

3   Courses of action

- mentor for Ellie
- own room
- reschedule of timetable
- head of department's role reviewed
- reschedule of work allocation
- discipline
- outside help
- courses
- creation of a staff development group

4   Decisions

- consultation
- counselling of Ellie – staff development group
- provide own room for Ellie
- set agreed targets within a timeframe
- provide INSET for Ellie and head of department

5   Action

- conduct 'interviews'
- reallocation of timetable
- meet targets
- organise 'INSET'
- review action

Figure 2.7 Ellie Crowther: recommendations of group 1

There are other human resources outside schools and industrial organisations which can be monitored to see if they will yield ideas and
experience which teachers in middle management positions can use to
augment their management skills. This is what I intend to do in the next

- Time made available for discussion on lesson content/schemes of work with head of department;
- PE department not allowed to use room for storage. Possible timetable changes to use *one* room as base;
- resources made available to rejuvenate wall displays; focus for lesson planning and boosting pupils' sense of purpose; incentives for higher personal standards in pupils (book covering);
- head of department and SMT back up removal or containment of troublesome pupils;
- pub/department lunches.

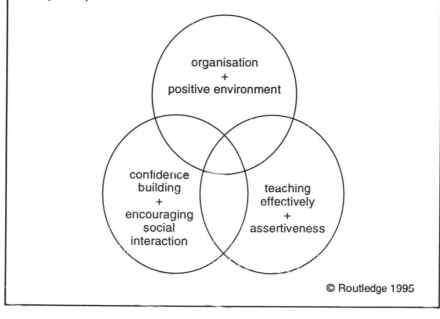

Figure 2.8 Ellie Crowther: recommendations of group 2

chapter, when the focus of the discussion is on a framework of management theories.

Chapter 3

A framework of management theories

This chapter will help the reader achieve the following objectives:

- learning the concepts and language of management;
- clarifying the concepts of management;
- learning how to motivate older and more experienced colleagues;
- learning how to motivate disaffected colleagues.

It will also enable readers to gain a relevant and useful theoretical framework for developing practical approaches to effective management. By effective management I mean three things:

- the optimum use and development of resources such as people, money, equipment, buildings, materials, time and space;
- using and developing specific skills, which include defining objectives, planning, organising, coordinating, listening, decision making, and reviewing the work of individuals and teams;
- achieving specified objectives.

THE CONCEPTS AND LANGUAGE OF MANAGEMENT

The following two theories will be useful in helping readers learn some of the concepts and language of management and clarify their ideas about management.

Adair's 'Three Circles Model'

The first theory to be discussed was formulated by John Adair (1983), who was for some time a senior lecturer at the Royal Military Academy, Sandhurst. Since then he has been a very active management consultant, and his approach to the management of staff has been strongly supported over a number of years by the Industrial Society, for whom he has presented many training programmes. His approach is known as 'Action-Centred Leadership' (ACL) or the 'Three Circles Model'. His essential

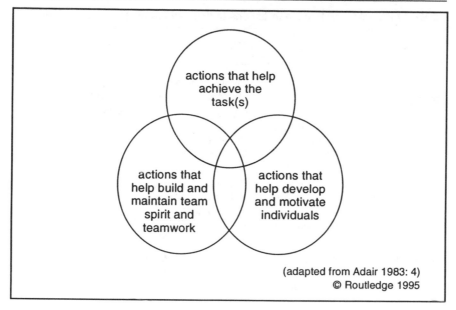

actions that help
achieve the
task(s)

actions that
help build and
maintain team
spirit and
teamwork

actions that
help develop
and motivate
individuals

(adapted from Adair 1983: 4)
© Routledge 1995

Figure 3.1 The Three Circles Model

belief is that for the effective management of staff, the team leader must attach equal importance to three essential factors:

- the task;
- the team;
- the individuals in the team.

One of my course members has given a clear example of a deputy head not following Adair's guidelines:

> The LEA tutorial skills course was introduced into my school. If we are to relate the actions of the deputy head to Adair's three circles theory, we can see that it is quite miraculous that the team was able to handle the implementation of this course with such vigour and enthusiasm. The two lower circles were definitely not considered by this deputy in her approach to the team. As we can see by the implications of the integration of the three circles, it is vital that these three concerns are met if a task is to be achieved successfully, and with the interests of team members taken into consideration. This harmonious liaison was not achieved in the implementation of the highly valuable course.

John Adair has also prepared a checklist of actions (see Table 3.1), which he has presented to members of his courses and readers of his books to help achieve the objectives in each of these circles. These actions are presented within a framework of key stages, from starting a task to

Table 3.1 Checklist of key stage actions to achieve management objectives

Key stages	Task	Team	Individual
Define objectives	Identify task and constraints	Involve the team, share commitment	Clarify objectives, gain acceptance
Plan	Establish priorities, check resources, decide, set standards	Consult, encourage ideas and actions, develop suggestions structure	Assess skills, set targets, delegate, persuade
Brief	Brief the team, check understanding	Answer questions, obtain feedback	Listen, enthuse
Support, monitor	Report progress, maintain standards, discipline	Coordinate, reconcile conflict	Advise, assist/ reassure, recognise effort, counsel
Evaluate	Summarise progress, review objectives, replan if necessary	Recognise success, learn from failure	Assess performance, appraise, guide and train

Source: adapted from Adair 1983: 77–128

completing it. Members of my courses say that this checklist provides invaluable basic guidelines for teachers starting out on their management careers and this detailed approach gives a clear indication of the strengths of John Adair's approach to management training.

The Blake and Mouton managerial grid

The second theory to be discussed also focuses on the behaviour of managers and makes recommendations about the types of behaviour most likely to lead to effective management of staff. This theory has been presented in many management training workshops and in several books by two American consultants, Robert Blake and Jane Mouton. It is based on the assumption that every manager should have two main concerns:

- achieving results
- people

In the Blake and Mouton presentation of their model these concerns are expressed as the axes of a grid and are numbered as in Figure 3.2. The management styles represented by the five numbered boxes in the grid are given the following descriptions by Blake and Mouton:

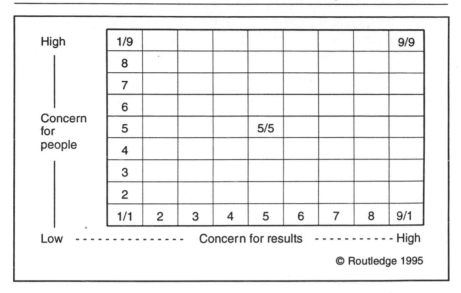

Figure 3.2 The Blake and Mouton managerial grid

1/1 Exertion of minimum effort to get required work done.
1/9 Thoughtful attention to needs of people for satisfying relation-
     ships leads to a comfortable friendly organisation atmosphere
     and work tempo.
9/1 Is extremely task orientated. Doesn't concern him/herself about
     other people's feelings.
5/5 Adequate team performance and attitudes to work maintained at
     satisfactory level. Conscientious rather than creative or innovative.
9/9 Work accomplishment is from committed people who have rela-
     tionships of respect and trust. Involves staff in decisions which
     affect them. Helps team to identify objectives and achieve them.

                          (Blake and Mouton 1985: 10)

One of my students recently added a further contribution to the description of the 9/1 approach to staff management: 'A 9/1 leadership style in
education is likely to result in promotion for the individual concerned. In
many schools the 9/1 style is easily identified as the deputy head in
charge of timetabling.'

   It would be good practice for readers to make further contributions to
these styles based upon their experience, and to think of colleagues they
have worked with or been managed by who seem to identify with these
styles. Readers might also like to consider which styles they use every
day. My course members tell me their styles move in the grid vertically,
horizontally and diagonally several times a day!

To help readers with this exploration, Figure 3.3 lists the various characteristics associated with the five styles. Using this checklist, readers should draw a profile on the grid of their range of management styles on a day or during a week.

Style 1/1

1   Passive behaviour
2   Does no more than required
3   Resists change

Style 1/9

4   Avoids open conflict – smooths and coaxes
5   If the school is 'happy' that is all that matters
6   Praises achievement to the point of flattering
7   Glosses over slackness or poor performance
8   Tends towards 'management by committee'

Style 9/1

9   Wants things done his or her way
10   'Tells' rather than 'listens'
11   Doesn't worry too much about other people's feelings or opinions
12   Aggressive if challenged
13   'Drives' things ahead
14   Checks up on staff

Style 5/5

15   Goes 'by the book'
16   Maintains the existing system
17   Conscientious rather than creative or innovative
18   Steady

Style 9/9

19   Agrees goals and expects achievement
20   Monitors performance against goals
21   Helps staff members to find solutions to poor performance
22   Faces up to conflict calmly
23   Agrees and monitors action plans
24   Involves staff in decisions which affect them
25   Delegates clearly
26   Takes decisions as and when needed

(adapted from Blake and Mouton 1985)
© Routledge 1995

Figure 3.3 Checklist of the characteristics of management styles

MOTIVATING OLDER, MORE EXPERIENCED OR DISAFFECTED COLLEAGUES

This section will present two theories which will help readers learn how to motivate older, more experienced or disaffected colleagues.

Before discussing the main proposals of these theories, it is important to give my definition of 'motivation', so that readers are clear about my concept. Motivation is the will to make effective effort. Managers responsible for motivating staff have two major concerns:

- to create and sustain in staff the will to work effectively;
- to share their will to work effectively.

Maslow's 'Staircase Model of Motivation'

The first theory presented here suggests that these two concerns can be met by satisfying the needs of staff and managers, for if managers lose their will to make an effective effort at work it is very unlikely that they will motivate their staff. This theory, known as Maslow's 'Staircase Model of Motivation', is outlined in Figure 3.4. The American psychologist Maslow proposed in his publications during the Second World War (Maslow 1943) that most people's needs were satisfied in an ascending order through the staircase, and he believed that they are motivated to attempt to satisfy the higher needs only when the lower level needs are no longer demanding attention. Teachers on my courses appear to be well aware of the relevance of Maslow's theory for certain situations in school – for example, when their fears of redundancy or redeployment become strong or when a school is under the threat of closure. Staff behaviour changes as teachers become preoccupied with job security. They become unwilling or unable to concern themselves with other aspects of their work situation, such as improving teamwork, achieving targets or even their own professional development. One course member reported some of the effects of the withdrawal of feelings of security, which seem to fit in quite well with Maslow's theory for staff in a closing school:

> In a closing school in which I worked, the head ran a good team which worked well and smoothly, but she could not help them overcome their demoralisation at closure, mainly I think because she identified herself with the sense of failure that closure brings. The whole situation became one of back-biting and nastiness and staff felt increasingly desperate to get other jobs, in many cases taking jobs for the sake of it and being unhappy. The whole closure was viewed as a disaster and not as an opportunity for self-appraisal and personal development.

It is important when considering the relevance of this theory of staff motivation not to take the hierarchy of needs as a fixed order of successive

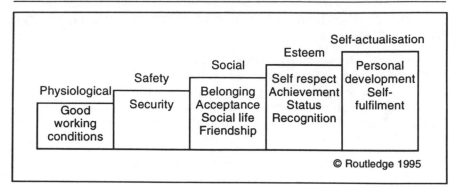

Figure 3.4 Maslow's staircase model of motivation

stages. Maslow himself warned his readers about this possibility: 'We have spoken so far as if this hierarchy were a fixed order but actually it is not nearly as rigid as we may have implied' (Maslow 1943: 46).

It is also important for readers to note the following comments of members of my courses. They report that they have differing orders of need satisfaction throughout the year – one head of year recently noted that his need for recognition is greatest towards the end of the summer term, when he is seeking to build up his motivation for the following academic year! Course members also state that they are highly motivated to perform well at work even though there is little sense of belonging and few opportunities for enhancing their self-esteem. They also claim that if they are enabled to find achievement and self-fulfilment at work they and their colleagues have a strong will to make an effective effort, despite the poor physical appearance of classrooms and schools.

These members are using Maslow's theory not as a blueprint but rather as ground rules for developing their understanding of how to motivate themselves and their colleagues, including older and more experienced colleagues and those who are disaffected. Readers, too, should use Maslow's theory in this way.

Herzberg's 'Two Factor Theory'

The second theory is Herzberg's 'Two Factor Theory'. He investigated these factors by asking engineers, accountants and managers in a wide range of industries in the USA to complete a questionnaire (Herzberg 1968: 132). One part asked them to report two recent incidents which made them feel well satisfied with their job and encouraged them to contribute even more. They were also asked to report two recent incidents which had interfered with their efforts to carry out their job effectively and produced feelings of job dissatisfaction.

When Herzberg analysed these results he found that the items most likely to cause job dissatisfaction included:

Ill-advised management decisions, ham-stringing procedures, or red-tape, union activities, management apathy towards problems or needs, delay or incomplete instructions and information, interference in the management of one's own operations, being by-passed in decisions affecting the job and having requests or recommendations turned down. Herzberg called these the hygiene factors because of their effects on the well-being of employees.

(Cotgrove, Dunham and Vamplew 1971: 36)

The factors most likely to encourage increased job satisfaction and effort were identified by Herzberg as achievement, recognition, job interest, responsibility and advancement. He proposes that these are the significant motivators, and he seems to imply that they are of equal importance. My investigations into these motivators with members of my teachers' courses and in my management workshops in industry suggest that they may have different importance for different people.

During each course and workshop members are asked to put the motivators in rank order of importance to them at that time and to add any others which Herzberg did not identify. It appears from these results, from 164 teachers in 18 groups since October 1987, that the most powerful motivators for the majority of course members have been job interest and achievement. The weakest motivator has been advancement. The middle-strength motivators, on the whole, have been responsibility and recognition. But these results also indicate that some groups did not follow this general trend. Job interest and achievement were placed only third in the rank order of two groups, which put responsibility and recognition at the top. The need for great care in drawing conclusions about what motivates teachers becomes even more apparent if the results from a single group are examined. This was the first group to be asked to give their rank orders of the Herzberg motivators in October 1987. In this group of 26 teachers, most of whom at that time had not been appointed to middle management posts, each motivator appeared at the top of at least one teacher's rank order and each motivator (apart from recognition) at the bottom of at least one!

A later course of 17 teachers expressed the idea that motivators probably varied for male and female teachers, so that hypothesis was tested. The results, shown in Table 3.2, suggest it might not be safe for middle and senior managers to assume that there are different motivators for the male and female members of staff!

But they may be on safer ground if they work on the assumption that most teachers will respond positively, with a strong will to contribute their effective effort, to interesting situations which enable them to feel a

Table 3.2 Motivators for male and female teachers

Motivators	Male	Female
Responsibility	2nd	2nd
Achievement	3rd	3rd
Job interest	1st	1st
Advancement	5th	5th
Recognition	4th	4th

great sense of achievement. These powerful motivating experiences at work will be reinforced for some colleagues by situations which enable them to accept responsibility and which bring recognition for their contributions.

These work experiences may put staff under considerable pressure but they may also be perceived as sources of job satisfaction. Some of the specific situations which bring into operation these strong motivators have been reported by teachers in my workshops. They include:

- the general 'business' of the day and the variety of tasks to get through;
- preparation and implementation of new teaching methods and topics not taught before;
- efficient use of resources;
- organising events/programmes within set time limits;
- working with students on constantly changing topics/projects;
- researching the subject;
- variety, the need to switch from one job to another and back again quickly, or to juggle several things simultaneously;
- designing a course;
- delivery of a difficult concept.

These activities might not be sources of job satisfaction for readers, so it would be a valuable review exercise for readers to identify those situations, experiences or activities which bring considerable job satisfaction to them and which strengthen their will to effective effort. To complete the exercise readers should also put the Herzberg motivators in rank order of importance to them at the present time, using his definitions as shown in Table 3.3.

Herzberg's theory suggests that managers' jobs have important situational responsibilities: to promote the optimum environment for the use and development of motivators, and to reduce the effects of demotivators. For members of my management workshops in industry, demotivators include the lack of:

1 consultation;
2 appreciation;
3 communication;
4 respect;
5 recognition;
6 flexibility on the part of senior management.

These demotivators are in rank order of importance from the top down.

Table 3.3 Herzberg's definitions of motivators

Motivator	Herzberg's definition
Achievement	Sense of bringing something to a successful conclusion, completing a job, solving a problem, making a successful sale. The sense of achievement is in proportion to the size of the challenge.
Recognition	Acknowledgement of a person's contribution; appreciation of work by management or colleagues; rewards for merits.
Job interest	Intrinsic appeal of job; variety rather than repetition; holds interest and is not monotonous or boring.
Responsibility	Being allowed to use discretion at work; shown trust by management; having authority to make decisions; accountable for the work of others.
Advancement	Promotion in status or job, or the prospect of it.

THE SITUATIONAL ASPECTS OF MANAGEMENT

The importance of the situational aspects of management is also strongly stated in the last management perspective I want to discuss in this chapter. This consists of a number of related theories which are given various titles: Contingency, Best-fit, Situational, Principle of Appropriate Leadership. The members of my Bristol University courses for middle managers have expressed considerable support for this general management perspective, as the following statements indicate:

- '"High flex" managers are willing to accept a variety of styles of management, varying degrees of participation and an assortment of control techniques. Appropriateness is their only test.'
- 'It is the nature of the circumstances surrounding the management tasks that has a causative effect on management style. This is put forward in contrast to the idea that a manager may have "free selection" of a particular style.'
- 'The lesson to be drawn from both the writer's survey and the more extensive research of others is that Fiedler's contingency theory is a particularly relevant theory of educational organisations.'

Fiedler's contingency theory

Fiedler emphasises the importance of three situational factors which managers must be sensitive to, and adapt their styles of management to, if they are to be effective (Fiedler and Chemers 1984: 57). These are:

- group atmosphere, the most important of the three, consisting of the feelings of trust, respect, liking and loyalty which members have for each other and for their manager;
- the degree of structure or flexibility involved in the performance of the tasks;
- the power inherent in the manager's position in the organisation.

Tannenbaum and Schmidt's theory

Flexibility and adaptability are also key requirements for management effectiveness as recommended by Tannenbaum and Schmidt (1973). They suggest that there are three sets of factors which determine the effectiveness of management, namely:

- forces in manager;
- forces in team members;
- forces in the situation.

Forces in managers include their:

- system of values – for instance, how strongly do they feel that individuals should have a share in making the decisions?
- confidence in the team members;
- leadership inclinations – there are some managers who seem to act more comfortably and naturally in a highly directive way, while other managers seem to work more comfortably in a more non-directive way;
- feelings of security – some managers have a greater need than others for predictability and stability, and may be less able to tolerate the uncertainty of allowing team members to participate in making decisions;
- physical and mental well-being.

Forces in team members include their:

- need for independence or dependence;
- interest in the work and organisation;
- expectations of management, for:

  Persons who have come to expect strong management and are suddenly confronted with the request to share more fully in decision-making are often upset by this new experience. On the other hand persons who have enjoyed a considerable amount of freedom resent the boss who begins to make all the decisions.

(Tannenbaum and Schmidt 1973: 178)

Forces in the situation include:

- the type of organisation – its size, customary management style patterns, values and traditions;
- the nature of the task;
- the expectations of senior management;
- time pressures.

Tannenbaum and Schmidt propound that successful managers are aware of these elements and are able to assess their strengths in different situations and decide which leadership styles are most appropriate (Tannenbaum and Schmidt 1973).

When my paper 'Appropriate leadership patterns', based on the work of Tannenbaum and Schmidt, was published (Dunham 1965) it included the type of organisation – its size, customary management styles, values and traditions – which now would be known as the school culture, but I did not appreciate its significance as possibly the most important situational variable. My perception has been sharpened and my understanding deepened by the letters, comments and reports of course members. A comment is included here which points to the constraints created by a key school culture element – senior management:

> Thank you very much for sending me the information regarding next week's course. I am particularly interested in the problems of staff management which must exist for many teachers who like myself feel hamstrung by the opinions, attitudes and actions of teachers at a more senior level. Although enjoying good personal relationships with the senior management team, the lack of a participatory style of 'government' frequently means that departmental initiatives will remain isolated or doomed to failure by the rather conservative views of the senior team or by their simple indifference to innovation. It would be easy to retreat into considering development within my direct sphere of responsibility (my department). However, it is obviously very difficult for such reforms to be of very much consequence as they are frequently dependent on general school structure and policies.
>
> I am very interested then in the relationship between the management style of a middle manager and that which exists within the school as a whole. Is this a constraint to departmental management, or is some degree of congruence not essential for effective management? I hope this makes sense!

SCHOOL CULTURE AND MANAGEMENT

One course member recently completed a project in her school in which she investigated by questionnaire possible changes in the culture of her school. She used Charles Handy's classification and description of four different types of culture: power, role, task and person (Handy 1988).

- *Power culture* has a central power figure surrounded by ever-widening circles of power and influence, just like a spider's web. The ability of the person in the centre is the key to understanding how these relatively small organisations function, because all direction and control radiate from the centre. Large organisations and power cultures do not provide a 'good fit'.
- *Role culture* is as carefully and thoroughly organised as a bureaucracy, which it closely resembles. It is managed by means of an organisation chart which defines the role occupants, their job descriptions, who they are responsible to, who they are responsible for, and so on. There are procedures for every eventuality. Role cultures provide stability and security. But if reorganisation or other changes affect the role culture there is often little flexibility or adaptability available from staff, who have been organised too well, too long.
- In *task culture*, specialist groups or teams come together to solve particular cross-curricular problems or achieve specific multi-disciplinary objectives. When they have completed their task they are changed or disbanded. Staff are enthusiastic contributors whatever their defined levels of responsibility, and there is a strong feeling of development – individual and organisational – as challenges are matched by effort. There are usually easy, friendly working relationships in this culture, with little attention being paid to hierarchy, age or status.
- *Person culture* puts the individual first and makes the organisation the resource for the individual's work. These favoured individuals are given (or take) a great deal of freedom to do their own thing. They are sometimes known as 'barons'.

The results of this head of year's study of her school are set out in Figure 3.5. It is interesting to note that these results show that all four culture changes have taken place since the Education Reform Act of 1988. The teacher gave further details of these changes:

Job descriptions were issued and the school formalised its management structure so that it now has strong features of role culture or line management. The job description removed role anomalies from my role as a tutor and in this sense was constructive; I was also aware that management control had been strengthened. The analysis [of Figure 3.5] confirms this. It shows that the strongest recent movement is towards a role culture and there is a slight movement towards power,

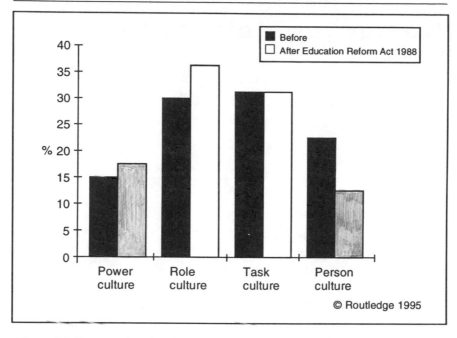

Legend:
- ■ Before
- □ After Education Reform Act 1988

(x-axis: Power culture, Role culture, Task culture, Person culture)

© Routledge 1995

Figure 3.5 Changes in school culture before and after the Education Reform Act 1988

with task culture, a dominant feature, remaining unchanged. The results show that my school has quite a strong tradition of both role and task culture with a significant degree of power culture but that person culture, previously stronger than power culture, is now weaker.

She gave some specific examples of task culture in her school:

The individual's role in task culture allows him to influence his surroundings and to have an impact upon his environment, to be an agent of change. In my school, for example, small working parties have been able to feed back suggestions for whole school changes in pastoral and curricular areas, on allocation of capitation, on accommodation and on discipline, on rewarding merit and on equal opportunities.

These developments towards an effective task culture are essential factors in the management of change. They rely on all team members being skilful at teamwork. The next chapter examines what these skills are and how they can be achieved.

Chapter 4

The management of teams and meetings

The objectives of this chapter include:

- recognising the benefits of teamwork;
- learning to build a team;
- learning to manage a team of colleagues;
- learning to chair a meeting.

These objectives can be achieved by considering the concepts contained in this chapter and by working through the teamwork exercises. It is important to have a clear view of the goals of teamwork, such as making collective decisions, generating ideas and providing emotional support. It is also important to be aware of the characteristics of effective teams, as well as of the 'building blocks' of successful team development and the essential roles which team members perform in effective teamwork. Guidelines for the coordinators of teams are offered, and practical exercises to develop greater awareness of behaviour within teams are provided. A particular concern of this chapter is the effective management of meetings; learning how to obtain a successful outcome and give satisfaction to the participants. Readers are also given guidelines on how to be effective members of teams and meetings as well as managers.

THE BENEFITS OF TEAMWORK

Successful team building depends upon a whole school policy to promote teamwork. This policy should seek to help all members of teaching and non-teaching staff to become aware that effective teamwork is essential if their school is to achieve its targets. At the end of the previous chapter, a report from a head of year indicated the importance in her school of working parties for the achievement of a wide range of organisational and curricular changes, including capitation allocation and equal opportunities. The following report from a head of faculty cites his belief in the significance of successful teamwork:

As head of a faculty at a time of radical change, one of my guiding principles has been to foster a team approach and a sense of working together within the faculty. We have been successful in implementing the National Curriculum and all the demands that came in its wake because we have planned and executed our strategies together. Change imposed from outside creates uncertainty and anxiety. I have sought to reduce stress by encouraging my colleagues to share their concerns and by always being willing to listen and offer positive comments. By fostering a feeling of mutual support and trust, I have tried to enable us to see change as positive, as an opportunity for improvement and greater job satisfaction: something to welcome rather than to fight against. In this way we have, for example, modified and developed our scheme of work to bring it into line with the National Curriculum, developed our assessment procedures to make them an integral part of our teaching practice, and worked on a faculty Equal Opportunities policy.

I had management experience of a different kind as the school IT Coordinator. The problems of trying to achieve changes right across the curriculum forced me to think hard about ways of achieving them. If permanent results are to be achieved it is important to establish clear goals leading to a set of specific objectives with deadlines for their completion. In this case I convened a task group with representatives from all areas of the school and we had some success in making different faculties take responsibility for the teaching of different aspects of IT. If such work is to be taken seriously, it needs to be given status by the involvement of senior management, and by the general expectation that proposals made will be implemented.

The head of faculty is right to attach so much importance to the involvement and commitment of senior management in the development of teamwork. When members of the 'top team' are perceived not to work well together, when there are major differences in the behaviour and attitudes to school concerns among them, when they do not cooperate or communicate as members of staff expect them to, they are creating barriers to effective teamwork in the school.

In these difficult and frustrating circumstances members of SMT need to be reminded, if necessary by middle management, of the notion of 'synergy; working together to create added value in thinking, services and achievements – the whole being greater than the sum of the parts' (Murgatroyd 1992: 196). They may need to be persuaded, together with colleagues at all levels of responsibility, of five possible benefits to the whole school, to pastoral and curricular teams and to individual members of staff when members are making a success of their teamwork. These five possibilities are:

- providing emotional support;
- coordinating interaction;
- inducting new members of staff or old members in new posts;
- generating ideas;
- making collective decisions.

The team is the major, and sometimes the only, source of emotional support for some colleagues in school. It enables staff to have a sense of belonging and of shared values and understanding. It satisfies staff needs for recognition, responsibility and achievement. The team has been called 'the emotional building block of the organisation' (Henley Distance Learning Ltd 1991: 80).

Effective teams coordinate the interaction of members of staff so that they are able to deal with complex information from many different directions and sources. It is not uncommon in school to see individuals who think they can 'go it alone' becoming overloaded with responsibilities, ineffective and eventually ill.

A third vital function of teams is induction, when new members learn the written and unwritten rules and norms of the organisation, so that within a short time they are working well and feeling good in the new environment. There may be whole school policy arrangements for the new members of the school community, including, it should be noted, supply and short-term contract staff. But curricular and pastoral teams have a vital part to play in helping newcomers fulfil the role to which they have been appointed. Teams can also help significantly with the successful adjustment of colleagues to new posts within the school.

Generating ideas is another major task of teams, and considerable benefit can be derived when all the members stimulate each other's thinking and creativity. The reader will probably have experience of the richness and breadth of the suggestions which can come from a brainstorming beginning to a problem-solving meeting.

The five arguments for advocating teamwork as an essential part of a school's Institutional Development Plan (IDP) may not match the specific benefits which the reader has experienced. It would therefore be good practice, before we consider some of the different criteria of effectiveness in teamwork, for the reader to compile a list of benefits which have been gained from good teamwork by:

- the whole school;
- curricular and pastoral teams;
- individual members of teaching and non-teaching staff.

The criteria now considered clearly suggest that to share these benefits certain guidelines for good practice in team management and membership must be followed. Two sets of guidelines have been provided by groups of course members. The first set identified:

- clarity of purpose and clearly defined roles;
- mutual support and motivation;
- getting the job done well
- evaluation, achievement and celebration.

The second set of guidelines for effective teamwork emphasised the importance of:

- clearly defined goals and roles;
- relaxed atmosphere – creative, friendly, trusting and humorous;
- evidence of achievement and recognition;
- willingness to listen and work together;
- being open-minded and flexible;
- taking positive action in implementing decisions.

Readers should now complete the same task that these course members were asked to accomplish: review their experience in school and non-school teams, and from the review make a list of the essential factors to form their own guidelines for effective teamwork.

These sets can now be compared with two lists taken from industry, in order to establish any similarities or differences. The first list, compiled by course members from one of my workshops in industry, came up with the following guidelines:

- clearly defined goals;
- optimum use of resources;
- recognition of strengths and weaknesses;
- monitoring of performance;
- open communication;
- flexibility;
- good interaction between members;
- job satisfaction;
- ability to cope with problems;
- successful induction.

The second list from industry is a comprehensive and detailed analysis of the characteristics of a successful team presented in an Industrial Society workshop:

- a high success rate – more often than not it achieves what it sets out to do;
- clear, challenging objectives – everyone in the team contributes to, shares understanding of, and is committed to the objectives;
- a coordinator (it may not always be the same person) who adjusts the

management style along a spectrum, from participative to autocratic, in the light of circumstances;

- a mix of people who contribute in different but complementary ways, thus achieving synergy (the team produces more than the sum of its individuals);
- a balance is struck between concern for the task (the 'what') and concern for the process (the 'how');
- a supportive atmosphere where people are happy to go at risk, say what they really think, develop one another's ideas and commit themselves to an agreed course of action, even though there may have been differences of opinion;
- learns from experience, both successes and failures, by reviewing its processes and constantly improving its own performance;
- works hard and plays hard – its members not only achieve challenging objectives but enjoy themselves as they do so.

These characteristics and guidelines can also be used as objectives for teams in school, to enable members to achieve optimum benefit from membership. The whole school, curricular and pastoral teams, and individuals will gain added value from effective team performance.

The next question to be considered is this: how can teams develop the skills and characteristics to achieve their objectives?

LEARNING TO BUILD A TEAM

My experience, in a considerable number of workshops and courses, suggests that teams in their development pass through a number of stages. Not all teams work their way through the same stages, or spend the same amount of time in each. Sometimes they regress and show behaviour and attitudes which they had previously discontinued. Each of these stages can be thought of as a developmental task for the team members.

Readers might profitably consider two approaches to the identification and description of the process of team building. The first framework comes from the Henley Management Centre. The management consultants there recognise five stages in the team building process:

- **Stage 1: Ritual sniffing**
  This part of the process is described as 'testing out and getting acquainted; the main concern is to find your place in relation to others and feelings and thoughts we usually keep hidden' (Henley Distance Learning Ltd 1991: 90).
- **Stage 2: Infighting**
  This stage is recognised as 'sorting out the pecking order by establishing the role of each member, sometimes causing conflict over control and dominance' (ibid.).

- **Stage 3: Experimentation**
  The management consultants advise us that 'some interesting changes occur: team members begin to care about the performance of the team and they are concerned enough to identify each other's strengths and weaknesses' (ibid.).
- **Stage 4: Effectiveness**
  At this stage 'relationships have been resolved, skills identified, communication improved and methods refined' (ibid.).
- **Stage 5: Maturity**
  'The mature team has the effective work methods of Stage 3 and the commitment from Stage 4, there is a deep level of comradeship, trust and friendship, and procedures are adapted to suit different needs' (ibid.).

The management consultants at Henley Management Centre suggest that this framework is relevant for an understanding of team development. But teachers need to review their experience in school to see if these stages can be recognised. Readers should now do this and, if possible, consult colleagues in order to get their comments.

The second approach to gaining an insight into team development is much more detailed than the Henley framework, but the main conclusions of the two are quite similar. The second approach, shown in Table 4.1, has been proposed by Woodcock (1979), and has been used very frequently in management training. It is recommended to the members of my teachers' courses as a good practice framework for understanding changes in behaviour and attitudes as team managers and members become more competent in their teamwork skills.

The achievement of Stages 3 and 4 can be very difficult and sometimes painful for managers and members. The management and interpersonal skills required are complex and need much preparation and practice for competency. So the management of a team of adults is a demanding and skilful professional task. Some of the barriers or demotivators to effective teamwork in their school teams have been identified recently by course members. They listed their main problems as:

- lack of information to make informed decisions;
- lack of individual commitment;
- personal issues, for example undisclosed concerns, aims etc.;
- unclear objectives;
- lack of participation by members;
- lack of success;
- lack of confidence;
- lack of interaction between members;
- lack of experience;
- lack of interest;
- lack of resources;

Table 4.1 Rating sheet for team development

Stage 1 characteristics	Stage 2 characteristics	Stage 3 characteristics	Stage 4 characteristics
Feelings not dealt with	Experimentation	Stage 2 with a more systematic approach – methodical working	Stages 2 and 3 plus high flexibility
The workplace is for work only	Risky issues debated, wider options debated	Agreed procedures	Appropriate leadership determined by situation
Established line prevails	Personal feelings raised	Established ground rules	Maximum use of energy and ability
No 'rocking the boat'	More inward looking		Basic principles considered, agreed and reviewed
Poor listening	Greater listening		Needs of all members met
Weakness covered up	More concern for others		Development a priority
Unclear objectives	Sometimes uncomfortable		
Low involvement in planning			
Bureaucracy			
Boss takes most decisions			

Source: adapted from Woodcock 1979

- lack of integration of roles;
- poor listening skills.

But course members have also reported that they have had experience of successful and productive groups in which very different behaviour patterns and attitudes are seen. Some of these are expressed in the following statements:

> I know what I have to do and the team's goals are clear.
> Everyone takes some responsibility for leadership.
> There is active participation by everyone.
> I feel appreciated and supported by others.
> Team members listen when I speak.
> Different opinions are respected.
> We enjoy working together.
>
> (Blanchard, Carew and Parisi-Carew 1992: 20)

LEARNING TO MANAGE A TEAM

So what can managers do to begin to reduce the negative and disheartening effects of teamwork demotivators? They should first make a list of motivators as guidelines for themselves. This is what a group of managers were invited to do on a recent management workshop. Their presentation to their colleagues in the workshop, shown in Figure 4.1, was well received.

M Make a point of being accessible to team members and have mutually agreed areas of responsibility.

O Opinions, contributions and experience should be valued.

T Treat colleagues as equals in the team and treat them as individuals in a professional capacity.

I Improve communication in teams by showing respect to others in the hope of reciprocal respect, not by showing position of authority.

V Value team and individuals by fostering responsibility.

A Allocate time for planning and discussion.

T Team members appreciate praise and constructive criticism.

E Encourage initiative taking and the need to work together, that is, for all to contribute.

© Routledge 1995

Figure 4.1 How to MOTIVATE your team

My second suggestion to enable managers to recognise and remove the demotivators is to provide an opportunity for their teams to do a S.W.O.T analysis. The mnemonic stands for Strengths, Weaknesses, Opportunities and Threats. In my experience, teams benefit from this review. The value of the exercise is greater if weaknesses are seen as training needs, which should be linked to the opportunities to achieve them. Training needs should be related to indifferent team performance and poor management and organisation, as well as to the difficulties and incompetencies of individual members. Threats should be understood as factors outside the team which are likely to have an adverse effect on its performance or even survival.

My third suggestion is specifically related to the identification of the human resources which a team possesses, so that they can be used well. This method has been researched and tested over a number of years by Belbin (1981). His methods have been used in a number of organisations including ICI, Marks and Spencer, the BBC, Rank Xerox and Westland Helicopters. His meticulous observation and analysis of successful teamwork at the Management College at Henley over a period of seven years clearly indicated that in successful teams there are eight essential roles. A short description of each role is given on the next page.

- *Company worker*: practical organiser; turns ideas into actions to achieve tasks; disciplined and conservative.
- *Chairperson/coordinator*: keeps members aware of team's objectives; manages strengths and weaknesses of team members; facilitates contribution from all members; is a good listener and summariser; promotes decision making by team.
- *Shaper*: continually attempts to influence the team's objectives, discussions and decisions!
- *Innovator*: contributes many original ideas which sometimes may not be very practical.
- *Resource investigator*: has contacts outside the team and often outside the school for information, materials, volunteers, help and sometimes funding.
- *Monitor/evaluator*: is a critic rather than a creator; appears cool rather than enthusiastic; analyses problems and situations; evaluates members' ideas and suggestions so that the team is better placed to take balanced decisions.
- *Team worker*: fosters good team spirit; attempts to prevent and reduce any conflict between members; a good listener; is more likely to be concerned with the members' behaviour and feelings than with the team's results.
- *Completer/finisher*: is very concerned with meeting deadlines; corrects errors and any lack of attention to detail; often strong on forward planning.

Belbin concluded from his research that team members prefer certain roles because of their personality, training and experience (Belbin 1981). This conclusion matches my experience of using the Belbin role inventory. Members of my courses are invited to complete the inventory and to use the results to gain information about potential contributions from their team members in a short period of time, when the team is in its first stage of development.

Some teams have used this analysis to good effect and have reported several advantages, for example becoming immediately aware of their strengths and weaknesses. This benefit was demonstrated quite dramatically on a recent course, when a team with six members found that three of them had very strong preferences for the Shaper role! They accepted the validity of these results and set to work to use the members' contributions, instead of allowing them to be wasted in unproductive confrontations. A continuing source of strength for these teams is the presence of conscientious company workers. A recurring weakness is the comparatively few members who want to make a major Innovator contribution.

For readers who would like to identify their preferred team role profiles, the Belbin inventory is presented in Appendix 1. Whatever the result at the end of this self-review, please be assured that it need not be permanent! It is possible to learn to develop new role preferences and skills by observation and discussion of colleagues' teamwork.

After completing the inventory on Appendix 1, readers might like to relate their scores to the descriptions of the eight roles just given and they should compare their scores with the results of course members on seven middle managers' workshops, which are given in Table 4.2.

Table 4.2 Middle managers' scores on the Belbin inventory

Number of people	CW	CH	SH	IN	RI	ME	TW	CF
(14)	15	9.5	9.5	5.0	5.2	7.0	12	7.0
(16)	12	7.0	8.6	6.5	8.0	6.2	9.0	5.0
(20)	13	5.5	9.9	9.5	4.8	5.4	12.2	8.3
(9)	10.5	10.2	12.7	6.4	6.4	7.1	9.1	5.5
(17)	12.0	7.7	11	6.1	6.3	6.3	10	8.8
(18)	14.6	8.2	11	4.8	6.8	7.1	11.1	6.4
(18)	12.7	10.1	11.1	5.4	8.0	5.2	10.4	6.2
Average	12.8	8.0	10.5	10.5	6.7	6.3	10.5	6.7

CW:	Company worker	CH:	Chairperson/coordinator
SH:	Shaper	IN:	Innovator
RI:	Resource investigator	ME:	Monitor/evaluator
TW:	Team worker	CF:	Completer/finisher

As well as indicating the role preferences in teamwork of some middle managers, there is also a suggestion that different teams may be stronger or weaker in some potential role contributions. Managers need to be aware of these possibilities so that they can recognise the need to pay special attention to certain aspects of their teamwork – perhaps the generation of ideas, obtaining resources, monitoring and evaluating team activities, or paying sufficient attention to deadlines. Using the Belbin inventory, this knowledge can be obtained without any of the painful criticisms and recriminations which characterise a team finding out the hard way about its weaknesses in Stages 1 and 2 of the Henley Management Centre analysis of the team-building process. It is essential that all team members are aware of each other's strengths and weaknesses so that all members will have realistic expectations of each other's teamwork skills.

LEARNING TO CHAIR A MEETING

The strengths and weaknesses of teams can often be seen most clearly during team meetings. It is important, therefore, that we tackle the final objective of those given at the start of this chapter: how to chair a meeting. Meetings are important as one of the most significant 'performance indicators of a team's development and effectiveness' (Jay 1976: 5). They are equally, if not more, important as opportunities to enhance effective and satisfying teamwork. This happens as members share a growing fund of knowledge, experience, feelings and skills in decision making and problem solving. This fund is a team bank account into which members contribute their deposits of time, energy, learning, skills and feelings, and from which they make withdrawals. Meetings also encourage teamwork by strengthening commitment to the team's objectives, policies, decisions and actions. Members can become aware of the common ownership of problems and strategies in the face-to-face contact of a meeting.

Meetings can achieve the benefits of successful and supportive teamwork by good planning, clearly presented objectives, good organisation of the interaction between members, well-formulated decisions and actions, and follow-up procedures to check the effectiveness of decisions. It is a very important part of the role of both manager and team members to ensure that 'meetings are vehicles for communication and action rather than for confusion and frustration' (Everard and Morris 1985: 51).

Course members have made some excellent recommendations to the chairperson:

- arrange for suitable venues for meetings so that the environment will encourage participation by all the members;
- try to prevent the need for AOB by good planning of the agenda and effective feedback of information;
- accept that you are accountable to the members;
- work hard to give equal opportunities to everyone;
- clearly mark the items on the agenda which require decisions;
- encourage members to attend only those meetings or parts of meetings which are relevant to them;
- have a built-in review system on objectives and decisions;
- ensure that you are a good facilitator, that you regularly summarise the progress of the meeting and that you are aware of the time factor.

These course members followed up their final recommendation in this list by providing guidelines to be a good facilitator:

- clarify objectives;
- emphasise equality of each member;
- be prepared to put forward your own opinions to start the ball rolling. Be honest yourself to encourage others to be so;
- encourage contributions by verbal and non-verbal behaviour, such as eye contact;

- encourage members to listen to each other's contributions by listening well yourself;
- praise people for their contributions;
- regularly review what has been said;
- ask open-ended questions such as: 'What are the major pressures we have?';
- sum up to conclude and check back with the team that you are reflecting their views;
- ensure that recommendations are written on large sheets of paper and displayed;
- thank team members;
- congratulate yourself on a job well done.

Very helpful recommendations have also been made by primary school staff who were members of workshops organised by Waters in the Education Management Unit at the Institute of Education, London University. They prepared 'Ten Commandments' for more effective meetings:

- Make sure that you need a meeting before you call one.
- People should be informed about the details of the meeting in advance and so have time to prepare themselves.
- Anyone should be able to place an item on the agenda and should be encouraged to do so.
- People should know when the meeting is to start and when it is to finish and punctuality must be observed by everyone.
- The role of the chair and scribe should rotate. The chair is responsible for the process of the meeting, including timekeeping, discipline, fairness, and sufficient formality. A good meeting needs structure and leadership. A strong chairperson will usually run an effective meeting. When the chair prefers a view or opinion she/he must make it clear that the role has temporarily changed.
- The time allocated to each item to be discussed is crucial – it should be enough to ensure that all points of view are expressed before final decisions are reached. This is a chair's responsibility.
- The shy, inexperienced and sometimes reluctant contributors should be encouraged to take a full part in the meeting. The loquacious, repetitive and dominant members should be effectively controlled. The subversive and otherwise undisciplined members should be dealt with skilfully. These are chair's responsibilities – but the support of the group will make the actions all the more effective.
- People should be invited in advance to make a leading statement on particular agenda items where they are known to be knowledgeable; a good discussion can then be launched.
- The scribe should be encouraged to use a flip chart on which the build-up of ideas, proposals and resolutions can be 'writ large'. The

various pages can be fixed to the wall as the meeting proceeds and reflect the history of the meeting.

- Crucial in this record must be the decisions reached, agreed and understood. Part of this adoption of a more systematic process will be the establishment of the action phase: 'Who will do what by when?'.

(Waters 1991: 1–2)

As the seventh commandment notes, effective team meetings require good practice in managing people as well as procedures. Jay has identified a number of problems concerned with members' behaviour in meetings and has put forward recommendations for resolving them (Jay 1976: 15). His suggestions are:

- Control the garrulous. If members take a long time and many words to say very little of relevance, the chairperson's sense of urgency should help indicate to them the need for brevity. The manager can also suggest that if they are going to take a long time it might be better for them to write a paper!
- Draw out the silent. Jay suggests that there are two kinds of silence which require management attention. These are:

  - the silence of diffidence;
  - the silence of hostility.

  The diffident member may have a valuable contribution to make to the discussion but may be nervous about the reaction of colleagues. The team leader can use eye contact and attention to encourage the member to speak. The silence of hostility, Jay suggests, 'is usually the symptom of some feeling of affront' (ibid.). It is a help to effective teamwork if the feelings of anger are expressed directly rather than maintained as an angry silence.

- Protect the weak. Junior members (because of inexperience, age, status or job) may have their contributions dismissed by their senior colleagues as not worthy of the team's time and interest. The team leader should commend their contributions 'by taking a written note of a point they make (always a plus for a member of a meeting) and referring to it again later in the discussion (a double-plus)' (ibid.). The manager can also promote the contributions of the less experienced, younger and junior members by asking for their contributions first before the big guns start firing.

These suggestions by Jay imply that managers should be proficient in quite complex interpersonal and group management skills. These are the concerns of the next chapter.

Chapter 5

Three key management skills

Members of my courses often ask the following questions relating to management skills:

- How can I learn the key management skills?
- How can I learn about relevant management techniques and how to adapt and modify them to suit my personal situation?
- How can I learn to increase my awareness of management skills?
- How can I learn to develop my management skills?
- How can I listen to others and develop my patience?

Experienced teachers have identified the following skills as essential for successful middle management: listening, delegating, decision making and problem solving, organising, motivating, communicating, planning, encouraging, supporting and evaluating.

Guidelines for motivating ourselves and our colleagues were discussed in the previous chapter. Recommendations for organising, communicating, planning, encouraging, supporting and evaluating will be presented in the following chapters. The present chapter is concerned with the skills of listening, decision making and delegating. Active listening is discussed and recommended. The characteristics of good listeners have been identified by my course members and readers will be encouraged to compile their own lists before learning some helpful listening techniques.

Good decision-making skills are also vital for effective management. The six steps in making a good decision are identified as: having clear objectives, gathering crucial facts, consulting people, making the decision, communicating the decision and follow-up. The characteristics of good decision makers are listed and the reader is asked to think of good decision makers and to identify their decision-making skills. Readers are also invited to analyse two decisions that they have taken recently – one successful and one unsuccessful – by using a checklist of 14 questions, including: What was my objective? How clear was my objective?. This part of the chapter ends with a list of recommendations for improving decision making.

Guidelines for effective delegating are then discussed, and the reasons why some managers are poor delegators are examined by considering the barriers to delegation. We look at the purpose and process of delegation and link it firmly with management coaching to encourage the professional development of managers themselves and their staff.

LISTENING

The importance of listening skills in effective management is clearly demonstrated in the following:

- The headteacher of a primary school described herself as a 'listening ear' when staff came to her with their personal, marital and emotional problems.
- The headteacher of another primary school reported: 'Other heads and the Advisory Service have provided valuable support in that they are prepared to take the time to listen while I talk out a problem with them. This is sometimes all it takes to solve a problem.'
- A head of year told me: 'My work involves continual listening to other people's problems, especially in a crisis.'
- The deputy head of a comprehensive school concluded his review of occupational stress with the following analysis:

> A final word about people – and listening to them. The single biggest frustration in my job is listening to people who take fifteen minutes to say what should take them five minutes. I hope one day to learn how to prevent them from doing this while still maintaining good relationships. Then again there is the rare colleague who, when listening to me, hears two sentences and understands the paragraph. Not only that, but they let me know they have understood and don't feel obliged to add their own comments. Life has its rewards!

These negative and positive feelings show how important it is to recognise the barriers to effective and satisfying listening. This conclusion is strongly supported by three management consultants who have written a useful, practical book on interviewing. From their wide experience they have recommended that part of becoming a good listener involves developing an awareness of the many obstacles to effective listening (Millar, Crute and Hargie 1992: 1356). They have identified the major barriers as:

- the listener is not able to give effective attention to the speaker's communication because of tiredness, illness or stress. Millar, Crute and Hargie make the important point that 'listening effectively is an exhausting exercise' (ibid.);

- the listener does not like or is indifferent to the speaker;
- the listener believes she/he has 'heard it all before';
- interruptions;
- a noisy environment.

My experience suggests other barriers:

- listening 'on the hoof' – like the deputy head who told me: 'I am literally pursued along corridors by staff';
- no time to listen – the same deputy head said: 'I have no breaks or lunch hour';
- the speaker may be known as the person who talks too much or who always repeats the same arguments whatever the focus of the discussion;
- the listener is attempting to 'juggle too many balls in the air' and is unable or unwilling to pay attention to the speaker.

Readers' experience may suggest other obstacles to effective listening, and at this point in the chapter it would be good practice to take a few minutes to identify them.

There are usually colleagues in school who do not seem to have any of these barriers and it is also a useful exercise to list their characteristics. Two groups of experienced teachers have completed this exercise recently and readers might like to compare their own views of the characteristics of the good listener with the following two lists:

Role model 1:

- understands beyond hearing;
- does not offer solutions but can change angle of thought;
- absorbs frustration and defuses tension;
- has the ability to concentrate attention solely on you;
- has the ability to make you feel valued;
- has the ability to give verbal and non-verbal encouragement;
- uses seating position to encourage two-way communication;
- has the ability to cope with silence;
- looks interested but not too interested;
- does not ask 'Why is that?' but 'How do you feel about that?';
- has a sense of humour;
- recognises that stillness in the listener is important;
- has integrity;
- is non-threatening in all senses;
- keeps to the speaker's agenda;
- provides a satisfactory ending to the conversation;
- never makes the speaker feel that the listener would rather be doing something else;
- enables the speaker to make decisions;

- enables the speaker to develop confidence.

Role model 2:

- uses non-verbal language to encourage the speaker, including: eye contact, facial expression, head movement, posture, gestures and body language;
- does not interrupt;
- concentrates on the speaker's verbal and non-verbal language;
- is non-judgemental;
- does not make a decision for the person;
- makes listening 'noises';
- summarises the main points.

These lists show that the effective listener receives and sends both verbal and non-verbal messages. According to these experienced teachers, the listener's messages should convey a willingness to learn. To achieve this objective, both verbal and non-verbal messages need to be congruent, complementary and in harmony. If they are not, it is unlikely that the objective will be achieved. This is the case when, for example, the questions and verbal responses of the listener show attention, interest and a willingness to understand, but the non-verbal language expresses boredom and impatience! Poor listening and poor communication also occur when the listener is nodding, looking interested and displaying the posture which transmits 'I am ready to receive' and 'I am receiving you loud and clear', but handles the verbal part of the transaction in a clumsy and inappropriate way, blocking instead of facilitating the interaction. So verbal listening techniques are an important part of the effective listener's skills.

Table 5.1 presents some of these key verbal skills, with a brief description of their purpose and how each can be used. In each case, to use them effectively requires much practice, patience and feedback.

These techniques and the complementary non-verbal methods of effective listening are also essential for the successful use of the second major management skill to be discussed in this chapter, which is decision making.

DECISION MAKING

The importance of developing the skill of decision making needs to be stated very strongly, because the well-being of all the members of the school community and even the survival of the school itself are dependent on the decision-making skills of senior and middle managers. When these skills are poor the consequences for staff can be quite negative. The following two reports indicate some of the problems caused by poor

Table 5.1 Key verbal listening skills

Types	Purpose	Examples
Clarifying	To get at additional facts. To help speaker explore all sides of a problem.	'Can you clarify this?' 'Do you mean this . . . ?' 'This is the problem as you see it now?'
Restatement	To check listener's meaning and interpretation with speaker's. To show the listener understands what the speaker is saying. To encourage the speaker to analyse other aspects of matter being considered and to discuss it with the listener.	'As I understand it then . . . ' 'This is what you have decided to do, and the reasons are . . . '
Reflective	To show that the listener understands how she feels about what the speaker is saying. To help the speaker evaluate his/her own feelings as expressed by someone else.	'You feel that . . . ' 'It was a shocking thing as you saw it.' 'You felt you didn't get a fair show.'
Summarising	To bring all the discussion into focus in terms of a summary. To serve as a springboard for further discussion on a new aspect or problem.	'These are the key ideas you have expressed.' 'If I understand how you feel about the situation . . . '

decision makers. They have been provided by the deputy heads at two primary schools:

> My main source of stress is the inconsistent nature of the headteacher. His inability to make decisions and abide by them means that staff, and myself in particular, never know quite where we are. Accompanying this, he will not delegate completely but always checks and changes any work undertaken. This does create stress situations with myself and other members of staff. At present the only way we can deal with this is to try to forget school in our own time.

> He was ten years younger than me and had no experience of working with infant or lower school junior age children. At first the staff were welcoming but gradually tired of watching what they considered unwise decisions. Many of the staff were very experienced teachers and resentment grew. I was often asked to voice their dissent and this put me in a very difficult situation.

We should also, however, try to gain insight into the causes as well as the effects of negative decision makers. To do this we need to be aware of all the curricular and organisational changes which have greatly altered the roles of teaching and non-teaching staff and members of middle and senior management during the 1980s and 1990s. A much more detailed account of these innovations, particularly those stemming from the Education Reform Acts, will be given in Chapters 9 and 10, but some of the problems experienced by those in middle-management positions are indicated in the following two reports. The first is by a head of house:

> As a head of house in a comprehensive school (14–18) I find one of the major stress situations occurs when important 'house business' has to be done when there is no real time to deal with it. One is faced with the choice of dealing with the problems immediately as soon as they come to light and thus neglecting one's other duties, namely teaching, or delaying dealing with the problems until time is available. Each solution, or the compromise which often results, brings some anxiety or stress. Feverish activity often results; lack of concentration and patience in lessons is also possible. In general I feel that classroom teaching must come first, thus one is left with problems to deal with 'as soon as possible' (this can result in things being rushed due to lack of time, or in significant delay occurring before any action is taken). There would seem to be no simple answers except unlimited free periods!

The second is by a head of department:

> During this academic year we have been faced with tremendous reorganisation plans in an attempt to implement the National Curriculum and keep the range of subjects, particularly classics, available to pupils. Heads of department for the first time have found themselves fighting for their subjects, trying to deal with overmanning in certain departments, having to devise new courses and find new resources. Their role has completely changed.

These changes and increasing pressures, which in my experience are representative of those affecting teachers in middle management posts, strongly suggest that decision making has become much more difficult and demanding for these teachers since the 1988 Education Reform Act. External constraints are causing major barriers to effective decision making.

Another possibility has to be taken into consideration, however. Poor decisions may also be made because of internal constraints in the minds of the decision makers. This is certainly the view of a team of experienced management consultants working in the Henley Management Centre. They claim to have recognised six such barriers (Henley Distance Learning Ltd 1991):

- *tunnel vision*: taking a narrow perspective during the creative and exploratory phases of the decision-making process;
- inability to handle complexity: being unable to cope with different kinds of information at the same time;
- lack of discipline: failing to impose logical and methodical thought processes;
- lack of creative capacity: being unable to generate novel perspectives and options;
- casual evaluation: failing to assess thoroughly the strengths and weak- nesses of each possible choice;
- indecision: avoiding taking a firm stand.

Readers may have had experience of working with and perhaps suffering from the effects of decisions made by people with these handicaps. The writer certainly has. But it is hoped that readers will also have had the experience, as the writer has, of working with and being encouraged and stimulated by good decision makers. Now our task is to find out more about the latter to see if we can define their essential characteristics. The members of my courses are asked to think of people, not necessarily in school, whom they would regard as good, successful, effective decision makers. It would be good practice if readers were to do this now, noting the essential characteristics of people they regard as good decision makers. Readers should then compare their lists with the following list, which is a summary of the analysis of course members. This list suggests that there are eight important indicators of effective and successful decision makers. They:

- are clear about objectives;
- are good communicators;
- are good listeners;
- are good time managers;
- ascertain all the facts of the situation;
- consider all possible options;
- consult those affected by the decision;
- are flexible before the decision and firm after it.

There is a further aspect of the good decision maker which is strongly emphasised by the management consultants at Henley Management Centre. In their view, effective decision making is an integrated process consisting of the following stages which might be called 'Six key steps in decision making':

- Objectives are frameworks which determine what is important or unimportant, relevant or irrelevant, urgent or not urgent.
- Data are the information which is needed about, for example, time factors, legal constraints, the people who should be consulted and who will be affected by the decision.

- Options are the possible choices.
- A decision is the 'best' choice in the circumstances.
- Action is the implementing of the decision.
- Feedback is the monitoring and evaluation of the results of the decision in the light of the first step.

The management consultants at Henley also emphasise a continuing professional development (CPD) approach to decision-making skills. They recommend that managers who want to improve their skills should study the strengths and inadequacies of their own approach. They should pay maximum attention to those steps in the decision-making process where they have weaknesses to overcome. This is important.

They provide an exercise to enable managers to consider their strengths and weaknesses (Henley Distance Learning 1991: 25) which I have adapted for use on my courses. In my version there are three parts to the exercise:

- a detailed account of two decisions taken recently;
- an analysis of those decisions;
- self-assessment of decision-making skills.

Members of my courses have been able to recognise a number of their training needs, such as:

- avoid thinking your way is best all the time;
- predict potential problems;
- be decisive;
- avoid tunnel vision;
- be sufficiently creative;
- be able to assess the strengths and weaknesses of each option;
- do not have too much consultation;
- be more disciplined and methodical;
- learn to trust other staff members;
- do not become aggravated with staff who do not think broadly/ quickly.
- control your impulsiveness;
- be careful not to be manipulative;
- be careful not to be bossy.

Recognising our training needs is a significant move forward towards their achievement. They become our 'one-at-a-time' goals, our personal continuing professional development programme. When readers have worked through the exercise and identified any training needs to improve decision making, it would be good practice to share these objectives with another person, so each can monitor the other's progress. Mutual support, congratulation and commiseration are powerful motivators!

Part 1: Detailed account of two recent decisions

Reflect on your work over the past three months and select two decisions that you have taken – one decision that you feel was 'right' and another you feel was (at least in part) 'wrong'. List the key points as follows:

- My 'right' decision:
- My 'wrong' decision:

Part 2: Analysis of decisions

Analyse both decisions by considering the following 14 questions:

- What was my objective?
- How clear was my objective?
- How well did I generate options for action?
- Did I recognise real limitations and constraints?
- Did I evaluate the options thoroughly?
- Were potential problems predicted?
- Was the implementation of the decision well planned?
- Could I validly be accused of 'tunnel vision'?
- How well did I handle complexity?
- Was my approach disciplined and methodical?
- Was I sufficiently creative?
- Did I assess the strengths and weaknesses of each option for action?
- Was I decisive?
- What, with hindsight, should have been done differently?

Part 3: Decision-making skills – self-evaluation

Look over the analysis you have just completed. It should tell you a great deal about your strengths and weaknesses as a decision maker. However, for the analysis to be really useful you must complete a consolidation exercise. Review your behaviour for both decisions as follows:

- My decision-making strengths are:
- My decision-making training needs are:

© Routledge 1995

Training material 5.1 Self-assessment of strengths and weaknesses in decision making

Another source of learning to satisfy training needs is to use a mentor, if one is already available in school, or to ask a member of senior or middle management to become one. The role of the mentor is to monitor the reader's decisions using the framework provided by the exercise in this chapter and to give valuable feedback. A third way, which may coincide with the second, is to use someone in school as a role model for developing decision-making skills.

These learning strategies are also very relevant for improving the third management skill to be discussed in this chapter – delegation.

DELEGATING

I will begin by trying to assess the importance of delegation and by suggesting some of the reasons for the low level of competence in delegation among middle and senior managers. The importance of effective delegating can be seen in the following report on some of the problems experienced by heads of department:

> The leadership behaviour of headteachers has been indicated by heads of department as a major source of stress. Their reports suggest that serious difficulties are caused by several facets of heads' management styles including their reluctance to delegate any responsibility for decision-making, a lack of communication between them and their middle management, failure to appreciate the needs of individual departments which results in bad timetabling, failure to provide clear job descriptions for heads of departments and their colleagues, inability to provide a clear style of decision-making, the appointment of staff without departmental consultation, the introduction of significant curricular changes without the participation of the departmental head, making timetable changes for staff without reference to the department, and finally the 'whittling away' of a department because of the head's negative opinion about the importance of the subject.
>
> (Dunham 1992: 86)

The strong negative impact of the non-delegating head on staff behaviour and feelings is shown in the following report from a deputy head in a comprehensive school:

> After a period of attempting to put forward my own ideas without success and discovering that an unpleasant scene could arise from any initiative action which had not been given the headteacher's minute scrutiny, one tended to fulfil one's administrative function mechanically and competently and concentrate on the teaching aspects of one's career, which was a negative solution. One felt resentful of being excluded and not gaining essential experience.

This style of management behaviour is not restricted to head teachers. It can be observed also in other members of the senior management team and in middle management. In my view, this is a widespread problem and before it can be rectified the causes need to be understood. It is hoped that this will lead, as it did with decision making, to the identification of training needs. My analysis of the barriers to the effective use of delegation is not presented in rank order of significance or frequency, but my experience suggests the following factors might be relevant:

- managers who believe that they have responsibilities which cannot be shared with colleagues (in the case of headteachers the claim is 'ultimate' responsibility);
- managers who are concerned about their prestige – if they are very status sensitive they will 'hang on' to tasks and responsibilities because they convey to colleagues, governors and parents significant symbols of power and authority in school;
- managers who demonstrate a lack of confidence and trust in colleagues when they are perceived to be incompetent and poorly motivated. Lack of trust is probably one of the biggest barriers to allowing colleagues to develop new skills through learning delegated tasks;
- managers who feel and say they are too busy and don't have enough time and don't want the hassles of sharing a task or entrusting a task to someone else;
- managers who are workaholics and want all the work they can 'get hold of'. They are as reluctant to let other people have parts of their job as they are to have holidays or weekends free from work;
- managers who may be unwilling to reduce their workload in case the governors or the headteacher begin to believe that they are less essential to the school's development plan and less indispensable than they were;
- managers who feel that nobody else can do the job, or any part of it, as well as they can and so perceive delegating as being too risky;
- managers who believe that they should know everything and should have a finger in everything that is happening in their team, department, subject or school.

There are also barriers caused by staff attitudes, such as:

- colleagues who believe that senior and middle managers should earn their high salaries by doing the work themselves: 'managers are paid to manage';
- colleagues who have been exposed to autocratic styles of management for a long time and are unwilling to change their expectations of senior and middle management. A secondary school head sent me a vivid and poignant report of this very difficult barrier:

Historically, the head here has made all the decisions, and getting people to accept my delegated authority is exhausting. I am unable to stop working, at school and at home, therefore I have a very barren social life, which is destructive to me. I think this comes from the fear of not covering all eventualities. Even the most difficult members of staff have been moved to comment on my voracity for work and how tired I sometimes seem, but I cannot stop. It's a drive to prove that I am doing what they expected. I get depressed when I blame myself for a failure and at the end of a long bad day. I've never contemplated not going to school but I go sometimes with apprehension.

(Dunham 1992: 42)

Barriers to effective delegation may also exist because attempts at delegation by managers may be perceived as weakness, laziness or incompetence. Another important consequence of having poor role models in school is that both staff and management may believe that delegating means off-loading jobs which managers want to relinquish. It is perceived by some staff as load-shedding, which should be resisted as strongly as possible, particularly as the pressures on staff have already been greatly increased by the apparently endless changes of the National Curriculum.

Delegating is more rarely perceived by staff and management as a two-way process in which the delegator learns how to coach and the delegatee has increased opportunities to learn about managerial responsibilities. In one of the schools where I work as a consultant a young science teacher responded positively to an invitation to staff from the deputy head, who has responsibility for primary school liaison, to join her planning team. She now has the responsibility, with support from the team and deputy head, for organising part of the primary school liaison day in the summer term.

For readers who want to share delegated tasks, whether as delegator or delegatee, the following guidelines will be helpful:

- Delegation is a two-way process. It is necessary for both parties to work carefully and sensitively towards full delegation of a task. The delegatee is helped and supported, with gradually decreasing monitoring, by the delegator.
- The delegated task is defined so that both parties are clear about expected outcomes, time, legal and financial constraints, and available resources. Methods of working are discussed but not defined, so that the delegatee can develop his/her ways of working, which may be different from those of the delegator.
- Thorough preparation is essential for both parties. At the planning meeting there needs to be explicit agreement about programmes of action, timetables and future monitoring discussions or meetings.

- Regular support and encouragement should be available in addition to the planned meetings. This again is a two-way process, each reassuring the other that the delegated task is being performed well!
- The planned meetings are review meetings, reviewing objectives, progress, limitations, training needs, resources and future plans. The inclusion of the hopes and fears of both parties is not irrelevant to the success of delegation.
- If delegation is not going well the reasons for the difficulties should be found without the delegator taking over and with much determination to learn from the experience. Again, even at the risk of 'overkill', it is important to emphasise that both parties should be involved in this learning process.

A checklist of possible causes of breakdown includes the following:

- ineffective listening skills of both parties;
- poor definition of delegated task;
- inadequate planning;
- procrastination, so that little has been achieved by the deadlines;
- lack of training;
- too much interference by the delegator;
- inadequate supervision by the delegator;
- lack of commitment by one or both parties;
- lack of trust by one or both parties.

These causes of breakdown can also be seen as the training needs of both parties. One effective way of satisfying these needs and gradually improving the quality of delegating skills is by management coaching. This has been widely recommended and used in industry because of its 'on-the-job' approach. Its method is to turn problem-based situations into learning situations by using the day-to-day contact between a manager and team members. This helps them develop in terms of knowledge, skills and attitudes. Through experience of management coaching, managers are becoming aware that 'coaching is a joint process through which the coach is as likely to learn as is the person being coached' (Singer 1981: 31).

This two-way interactionist approach is the essential style for professional development and training in the 1990s. To improve delegation by using management coaching, both parties need to be proficient in the skills of observing, listening, appraising, discussing and decision making. For Singer, 'the ability to listen well is perhaps the most important of the skills possessed by a coach' (Singer 1981: 77).

All of these skills have been discussed and promoted to realise the objectives set at the beginning of the chapter, which were to identify and develop key management skills and techniques. But these skills are not book-based. They are practical as well as conceptual. They are work-based. They need practice, practice and yet more practice to bring them up to the quality which is required for successful performance. This focus on training and professional development is continued in the next chapter, as we spotlight the integrated process of selection and induction.

Chapter 6

Continuing professional development: selection and induction

Teachers striving to fulfil management tasks have identified the following training needs:

- learning how to answer questions at interview;
- learning the skills of interviewing;
- discovering how to sell ourselves to present/future employers;
- learning staff selection skills;
- finding a means of professional development.

In this chapter readers will have the opportunity to learn how to achieve these objectives. They will be empowered to identify their needs, ambitions and skills, as well as review their present position and their strengths and training needs. They will be asked to consider their short- and long-term career goals, and which skills need to be developed to achieve them. And they will be asked to complete a practical exercise to identify the factors involved in applying for a promotional post which includes new directions, more responsibilities and financial improvement.

Readers will learn that selection is the starting point of professional development for teaching and non-teaching staff. They will also see the importance of strong links between selection and induction, for if these are weak the advantages of an effective and systematic selection process may be lost. Induction programmes for all external and internal appointments are essential.

REASONS FOR SEEKING PROMOTION TO A MANAGEMENT POST

The focus on professional development for readers is directed towards gaining a middle management post and developing the necessary knowledge, skills and attitudes to progress along the management career path. These goals involve teachers in making significant decisions about work choices and lifestyles. These choices have the important positive results of job satisfaction and the negative consequences caused by stress, which may affect teachers' lifestyles and their families.

The reasons for seeking promotion to a management post and undertaking a career in management should be regularly reviewed, together with realistic assessments of the advantages and disadvantages, the opportunities and threats of being a manager. The teachers on my courses who are seeking middle and senior management posts have identified the following reasons for wanting promotion:

- autonomy;
- new direction at work;
- more responsibilities;
- increased challenges;
- improvement in salary;
- more status;
- more power;
- a sense of achievement;
- more job satisfaction;
- less stress;
- to be valued more;
- to be more involved in making decisions;
- more interesting work.

Readers should compile their own list and compare it with this one. They should also ask middle and senior management colleagues to what extent their work enables them to achieve these objectives. If these managers are willing to offer further help they can be asked:

- What does your work involve?
- What parts of your work do you find satisfying?
- What pressures of your work cause the greatest problems?

These questions are part of a questionnaire staff are asked to complete to prepare an INSET workshop in their school. Three sets of answers from middle managers in a secondary school before a recent INSET day are presented in Figures 6.1, 6.2 and 6.3.

These reports indicate the advantages and disadvantages of, and the opportunities for, a satisfying and enjoyable work style for the middle managers in one particular school. The reports of the middle managers in readers' schools may be different, so it is important to obtain this information. It is also helpful to learn more about the work experience of management in other schools. Michael Marland has written very perceptively of the experience of stress:

Any responsibility post in a school is primarily concerned with facilitating the work of other adults. Most of the tasks described so far have not been concerned with the worries or strains of those other adults, and yet a teacher is likely to experience a variety of kinds of stress that

What does your work involve?

Maths teaching.
Staff development work – organising INSET, identifying needs, co-ordinating appraisal, and acting as an appraiser, new staff inductions and oversight, student teachers' coordination and oversight.
Monitoring the National Curriculum, Key Stage 3 coordination.
Membership of working groups of staff who are planning change.

Which parts of your work do you find satisfying and enjoyable?

I enjoy most of it. I like working with people generally, both staff and pupils. I enjoy some administration, when it is meaningful! I enjoy working with computers and take a pride in the finished products. I dislike having to respond to late management decisions when I have planned my day and have to re-schedule priorities.

What pressures of your work cause the greatest problems?

The effect on my family – divided loyalties – the feeling that I am letting them down. Doing the shopping, cooking and washing every weekend. No time to relax, just more work. The working load for Maths is very high. I just have too much to do and like to do it well. I find it difficult to do things properly.

© Routledge 1995

Figure 6.1 Answers to INSET questionnaire: report 1

What does your work involve?

Head of English: administration as well as responsibility for all aspects of running the department.

Which parts of your work do you find satisfying and enjoyable?

Teaching and one-to-one contact with individuals for counselling and so on. (I relish the teaching part of my job more and more!)

What pressures of your work cause the greatest problems?

Getting behind with organisation, such as marking in the English department, because of pressure elsewhere.
Other members of staff 'dumping' on me!

© Routledge 1995

Figure 6.2 Answers to INSET questionnaire: report 2

What does your work involve?

Head of department: normal administration of ordering books and equipment, pupil lists and progress, monitoring the progress and giving support to a probationer.
Form tutor: helping students' development and keeping their records up to date and accurate.

Which parts of your work do you find satisfying and enjoyable?

Most of the administration, if I have enough warning of deadlines so that I can comfortably achieve it before the appointed time.
Teaching in class and contact with the older pupils in a pastoral role.

What pressures of your work cause the greatest problems?

Trying to organise the Key Stage 3 curriculum.

© Routledge 1995

Figure 6.3 Answers to INSET questionnaire: report 3

are inherent in the profession. The management tasks must include helping those teachers cope with that stress. The responsibility holder, too, has additional stresses that come from work with other adults, often other teachers previously thought of as allies against difficult pupils, parents and the outside world. This kind of managerial stress often comes unexpectedly, and often goes deep and hurts. Teachers carrying responsibility are better able to cope with the stress in their managerial task if they can consciously work on it. Thus they have the double job of helping themselves and helping those for whom they are responsible.

(Marland 1986: 87)

My research (Dunham 1992) strongly supports this conclusion and my recommendations for strengthening stress management strategies are presented in Chapter 10.

ASSESSING READINESS FOR A MANAGERIAL ROLE

There are good reasons, then, for suggesting that there are many opportunities for professional and personal development as a middle and senior manager. But it is necessary to look very objectively at the risks involved in seeking and gaining promotion. It is essential that readers carry out an audit of management readiness by reviewing their strengths, training needs, opportunities and threats:

- *Strengths* should be seen in terms of the professional and personal experiences which have enabled readers to develop some of the skills which were identified in the previous chapter as essential for effective management.
- *Training needs* should be seen in terms of a lack of the experience which would have generated the required skills, knowledge and attitudes, as in the previous chapter I suggested analysing and identifying training needs for effective decision making. Perhaps the 'Aptitude for management' scale shown here might be of some assistance in your review. It has been adapted from a distance learning programme (Henley Distance Learning Ltd 1991).
- Readers should review their *opportunities* for the realisation of work and whole life goals, which include their values and beliefs as a manager.
- They should also identify any *threats* to the achievement of these goals, to job satisfaction or to personal or family well-being due to negative work experiences and stress as a manager.

HOW TO PURSUE A CAREER IN MANAGEMENT

Readers should now be in a position to draw up a comprehensive balance sheet of the advantages and disadvantages of being a manager. If they conclude after this analysis that they should continue with their career preference for management, the recommendations of careers counsellors could be of considerable value. These recommendations include the following guidelines:

- Teachers should be responsible for their own career development by being responsive to opportunities for taking on delegated responsibilities, by seeking opportunities to shadow parts of the mentor's role, by discussing their CVs and letters of application with senior managers, by getting job descriptions and person specifications for jobs similar to those for which they might apply in the near future.
- They should assess the skills which they have gained from their previous and present work experience and the training needs which are the targets for their professional development.
- They should plan the career paths they see for themselves and the targets they work towards as short-term and long-term goals. They should find out about relevant courses and qualifications which will give them personal and professional confidence and enhanced credibility for job applications.
- They should try not to be sidetracked into pathways which are not leading in the general career direction, even though they may be pleasant and comfortable! Readers should also accept that career goalposts may change and so career plans may have to be changed. Career

Assess your aptitude for management by answering these questions as honestly as you can. This activity is for your eyes only – so do not fool yourself!

Rate the statements on a scale of 1 to 5, where 1 means 'absolutely not true for me' and 5 means ' strongly true for me'.

- I like lots of variety at work and at home.
- I can change track very easily – I am flexible.
- I enjoy independence.
- I like responsibility.
- I enjoy making decisions.
- Making quick decisions does not worry me.
- I like to stretch myself.
- I enjoy setting objectives.
- I always set realistic targets.
- I invariably achieve the targets I set myself.
- I think I deserve the money I earn.
- I feel confident dealing with many different kinds of people.
- I am good at getting people to work well with me.
- I do not find it difficult to generate lots of new ideas.
- I am prepared to take responsibility for my actions and decisions.
- I enjoy taking risks.
- I can deal effectively with stress.
- Power does not go to my head.
- I am prepared to change tack if I am proved wrong.

Now add up your scores.

65 to 85	Most successful managers probably come into this group.
25 to 65	There is probably quite a lot for you to learn and think about in relation to the demands of management.
Below 25	Try the activity on a day when you are feeling more confident!

© Routledge 1995

Training material 6.1 Aptitude for management

hopes and expectations may come to a sudden halt because of redundancies and school closures or unemployment. Career plans may have to be delayed because only short-term contract work can be obtained. Career plans may be changed by family responsibilities.

These dips and breaks may make considerable demands on career management skills and help from career/adult guidance services may be necessary to get started again. But these four recommendations will be helpful both for readers whose career paths are difficult and for those with a smoother ride.

Managers have a great, but of course not a total, influence on the professional development of staff. Government policy decisions and initiatives formalised in Acts of Parliament in the 1980s and 1990s are setting stringent frameworks for professional development opportunities. New opportunities must therefore be found, and whatever is done to promote and foster the continuing professional development of staff must be done well to match the demands of unremitting curricular and organisational changes. 'Develop or die' has been a widely accepted policy statement for industrial organisations for a long time. It has not been thought to be at all relevant for educational organisations, but it is becoming more relevant as an epigram for schools. The essential rule is that school development will not happen if staff are not developing. If staff are developing professionally their school will successfully meet the demands of the turbulent 1990s. It is one of the prime tasks of management to see that this happens. It is every manager's task. It can be achieved by having effective programmes in four areas of staff management: selection, induction, appraisal and training. Each of these is a vital part in an integrated system of staff care and development. The rest of this chapter is concerned with selection and induction; Chapter 7 looks at appraisal and training.

STAFF SELECTION

Staff selection is a vital task for senior and middle management. It is the first crucial step in providing and promoting equal opportunities for staff development. It is essential if human-resource management is to be successful in school. Achieving good practice for governors, officers, headteachers and deputies in the management of selection should have top priority rating, not only because of the widely held perception that too few women and teachers from ethnic minorities are achieving senior positions, or because the contraction of promotion opportunities is keeping staff in the same school for much longer periods of time, or because salaries are the biggest item in a school's budget. There are considerable human costs, which can include stress for the person appointed and for his or her colleagues if selection procedures are faulty.

Causes of faulty selection procedures

A major reason for these faults in the selection of teachers has been proposed by Geoffrey Edwards, an adviser for primary and middle schools:

'Despite the unprecedented changes of the last few years, there are sufficient personal anecdotes circulating amongst teachers demonstrating that
staff appointment procedures have changed little in substance for 50
years or so' (Edwards 1993: 62). More weaknesses in staff selection have
been identified by members of my management courses. Three reports
show a number of different causes:

Report 1

It is difficult to imagine that a school which was actively concerned
about staff development, both for its own benefits in terms of a
happier, better motivated and efficient workforce, and also for the
benefit of the individual members of staff and their own professional
development, could not give priority to the selection process. There are
extremely persuasive and compelling arguments which all indicate
that an effective selection procedure should form the basis of a school's
organisational structure for staff development.

We have all had experience of teachers whose first months or even
years were marked by problems of a severity to cause their colleagues
to question the wisdom of the appointment but who, through
counselling, experience, maturity and so on, managed to become very
capable professionals who never had cause to look back. However, this
ignores the casualties who are forced to leave teaching, move schools
rapidly, or hide their unhappiness and even humiliation and live with
their problems. The superficial consequences for their schools of these
incorrect appointments are obvious to all, and the more senior the post,
the more wide-ranging and potentially damaging are the consequences.

If the selection procedure is failing, due to weakness in any of the
processes, from writing the job description to the final selection of
interviewees, then it is hardly surprising if staff development is un-
satisfactory.

Report 2

Sometimes schools slot more than one type of interview into the interview day. For example, during one interview day I was subjected to
the trauma of a thirty-minute group interview, two fifteen-minute
sessions with key panel members and a forty-five-minute finale with
eight selectors. These sessions were not particularly well planned, and
by the third session I was becoming concerned about the number of
times I had repeated myself to interviewers who had clearly not worked
out a comprehensive framework for the day.

Report 3

Once the letters of application and CVs have been received the
selectors should compare these with the job description and person
specification to identify suitable candidates. The long listing then takes
place and the references are requested. Selectors should ensure that the

referees are provided with a framework or structured questionnaire based on the job description and person specification which should also be sent to referees. Once the references have been received, the selectors should draw up a short-list and notify successful applicants of the date of their interview, taking care that each candidate is provided with a brief synopsis of the interview day(s) and additional data on transport services to the school, local accommodation and expense claims. From my own experience and from that of my colleagues at the school where I teach (see Table 6.1) evidence suggests that selectors do not normally make such thorough preparations for interview! In addition, my research reveals that many applicants for teaching posts are themselves guilty of insufficient preparation. Ideally, the selectors should have received some form of in-service training on interview technique, from their LEA or via their staff development programme, to assist them with a variety of skills, such as questioning, listening, showing interest, attempting to see the interviewee's point of view, observation and note taking. Five of the six interviewers who completed my questionnaire said they needed to become more skilful at questioning, whereas the sixth person wanted more guidance on how to develop individual interview criteria grids to enable candidates to be compared.

Table 6.1 Items made available before 18 interviews

Items/opportunities	Received		Not received		Not applicable; internal appointment	
	No.	%	No.	%	No.	%
Job description	17	94	1	6	–	–
Person specification	1	6	15	83	2	11
Background details about school and its catchment area	13	72	1	6	4	22
Information on how the interview day/s were to be organised	8	44	9	50	1	6
Tour of the school	13	72	1	6	4	22
Opportunity to talk to staff not involved in selection process	14	78	3	16	1	6

Number of interviewees who filled in a questionnaire – 12
Number of interviewers who filled in a questionnaire – 6

Total – 18

Good practice procedures for staff selection

The three reports just cited show how important it is, in reducing the chances of appointing an unsuitable headteacher or member of staff, to follow systematic, well-prepared procedures rather than to rely on personal experiences or what a very experienced interviewer has called 'gut-feel' decisions (Courtis 1988).

The good practice procedures consist of a series of stages, each of which is significant in determining the final decision for the appointment. These interdependent stages are:

- analysis of the needs of the organisation;
- analysis of the tasks performed by the postholder, leading to the preparation of the job description;
- analysis of the personality, qualifications, training, experience, skills and abilities of the person most likely to meet the requirements of the post: the person specification;
- preparation of the advertisement, which should be a brief summary of the job description and person specification. The complete description and specification should be sent to enquirers about the post. In this way some self-guidance takes place if teachers decide that the post is not suitable for them. This makes the next stage more manageable;
- long-listing and short-listing, using information supplied by the candidates and their referees. A structured questionnaire should be used for taking up references based on the job description and person specification, which should also be sent to the referees;
- interviewing, in which all the people involved (interviewers and interviewees) are well prepared for their respective contributions;
- decision making in relation to the job description and person specification rather than a comparison of the candidates. Disappointed external candidates are grateful for feed-back on the reasons for their non-appointment and on their interviewing style. The internal candidates who are not appointed need more than one post-interview session to cope effectively and productively with their disappointment;
- analysis of the interviews by the interviewer and possibly by the interviewees;
- follow-up of the person appointed by regular review interviews, using the job description as the framework.

Becoming a successful interviewer

If these nine steps are integrated into a school's selection programme the three conditions which are essential for the improvement of selection and interviewing skills will be fulfilled. These three vital requirements are that interviewers should:

- know how to prepare a job description and a person specification;
- know how to assess the key factors in the candidates by the use of a systematic interview;

- be aware of the importance of regularly reviewing the effectiveness of their selection procedures.

Knowing how to prepare a job description and a person specification

The preparation of a job description is necessary for the selectors and for the guidance of potential candidates. The job description should give potential applicants the information needed for their decision whether or not to apply. It should include up-to-date, realistic and detailed information about the purpose, scope, duties and responsibilities of the vacant post.

The information from which a job description is prepared can be obtained in two ways. It can be sought in an exit interview with the person whose departure is causing the vacancy or, for example, it can be obtained from discussions with a number of people who are holding appointments similar to the one which is to be made.

When the job description has been written it should be used in preparing the person specification. This delineates the qualifications, specific skills and knowledge, experience, training and personal attributes of the person most likely to meet the requirements and demands of the post. These categories can be qualified by identifying those that are essential or desirable for a particular job. The final category – personal attributes – should now be receiving more attention in appointments for a number of reasons, one of which has been identified by Humphreys: 'The impact of the new individual on an existing work group and vice-versa can be vital in many situations. Some attempt must be made to analyse the chemistry of the situation' (Humphreys 1983: 881).

More attention should also be given to another personal attribute, that is the stress-management strategy, which is essential for management positions. Humphreys again singles out this attribute for particular attention: 'This question of stress and the individual's capacity to absorb stress is very important especially at certain decision making levels' (Humphreys 1983: 881).

The importance of interpersonal relationships in a person specification for a management post can be seen quite clearly in Figure 6.4. This list was sent by a secondary school to prospective applicants for a middle management appointment.

When the person specification and job description are complete they can be used in the advertisement for the post. When the shortlist has been prepared by scrutinising the application forms, CVs and/or letters of application, the job description and person specification can also be used to guide the questions which are asked during the interview. If the interview is conducted on this framework it will follow the second of my three recommendations for the improvement of selection skills.

Applicants should be:

- committed to the roles and responsibilities outlined in the job description;
- capable of managing a team of year staff;
- capable of working as part of a head of year's team;
- able to organise large groups of pupils;
- able to plan activities for large groups of pupils;
- well organised;
- effective classroom teachers with sound pastoral experience;
- able to communicate with staff at all levels;
- able to foster and maintain good relations with parents in a variety of situations;
- able to liaise effectively with heads of faculties over relevant curricular matters;
- informed of the part outside agencies play in the welfare of pupils;
- aware of the role of the head of year and confident of understanding when to delegate and when to refer.

© Routledge 1995

Figure 6.4 Selection criteria for head of year

Knowing how to assess key factors by the use of a systematic interview

The purpose of the interview is not only to confirm what has been written on the application form; it should also provide an opportunity to amplify this information and to find out about the important but less tangible factors of motivation, attitudes and expectations. These aspects of personality can be explored in a reasonably satisfactory manner if the interviewers pay attention to the main principles of successful interviewing, which have been identified by experienced practitioners. These guidelines may be very briefly summarised in eight points:

- The chairperson of the interviewing panel clearly introduces the members.
- The purpose of the interview is stated.
- Rapport is established in an atmosphere of informality in a private, comfortable room in which telephone calls and other interruptions are avoided. After the introduction the interviewers begin discussing an interesting topic from the application form.
- All questions are asked in a manner which encourages the applicant to talk freely. Questions that evoke a 'yes' or 'no' answer are not helpful. The interviewers should not feel it is necessary to speak if the applicant pauses. The interviewers' silence implies that more information is needed and, given time, the interviewee usually supplies it.

- The candidate should be listened to attentively and should not be interrupted.
- He or she should do most of the talking which occurs in the interview.
- When the interview is being ended the candidate should be given some indication of future action so that he or she is not left wondering what happens next. The interview should be closed by following an essential recommendation from a very experienced professional interviewer: 'End the interview in the same friendly manner in which it began and, no matter what the nature of the interview, always try to leave the interviewees with their dignity and self-esteem intact' (Gratus 1988: 93).
- As soon as the candidate has left the room the task of evaluating the information should be undertaken. A summary of the information should be written into the framework of the job description and person specification. The decision is made in relation to job requirements and not by comparison with other candidates. The unsuccessful applicants should be given an opportunity to discuss with a member of the interviewing panel the reasons for their non-appointment and suggestions for the improvement of any weaknesses which were observed in their application or interview.

When these tasks have been completed the interviewers should follow my third recommendation for the improvement of selection skills:

Being aware of the importance of regular reviews of selection interviews

They will be able to carry out this interview evaluation if they use a checklist of the various aspects of an interview which require attention if it is to be successful. There are a number of questions which are relevant for this purpose:

- How well did the interviewers receive the interviewee and did they put him or her at ease?
- How successfully did the interviewers open the interview? Did they get to the important topics quickly?
- How successful were the interviewers in moving from one topic to another? Did they direct the conversation unobtrusively? Did they prevent the interviewee from wasting time? Did the changes of subject seem abrupt?
- How successful were the interviewers in closing the interview? Did they close as soon as all the necessary business had been completed? Did the close appear natural and satisfactory to the interviewee? Did it seem abrupt?

Interviewers might like to use the self-review table on the next page.

	Very effective	Adequate	Ineffective
Layout of the room			
Introduction and starting interviews			
Suitability of questions asked			
Listening skills			
Panel teamwork			
Equal opportunities offered			
End of interview			
Any other comments			

© Routledge 1995

Training material 6.2 Interviewing panel self-review

Formal interviews are normally accompanied by informal pre-interview sessions typified by tours of the school or discussions with the staff in the department interviewees are wishing to join. The staff involved in these sessions may be asked to pass on their views of the candidates to the interview panel. Some schools also include tests and simulations in the interview day/s. Candidates may be asked to teach a lesson, to tackle a decision-making exercise or to solve a hypothetical problem. Regardless of whether the interview day contains a wide range of activities or only a few, it is essential that the selectors compile a comprehensive activity plan to ensure that interviewees and interviewers gain by the experience. Each session requires clear objectives to be set to ensure that interviewers avoid wasting time in covering the same ground. These plans and procedures should also be reviewed.

Becoming a successful interviewee

These recommendations suggest that selecting staff effectively to achieve a secure basis for their professional development requires the use of an extensive range of management skills. But additional skills were also requested in the objectives set out at the beginning of this chapter, including those related to being selected rather than selecting. Two of these were:

- learning how to answer questions at interview;
- understanding the practicalities of moving forward professionally.

The skills to achieve these objectives are also wide ranging. One set of skills is concerned with being an effective and successful interviewee. The following guidelines were provided by course members.

- be aware of the importance of non-verbal communication in interviews;
- answer honestly;
- think before you begin to answer a question;
- be precise and decisive where possible in answering questions;
- ensure the answers you provide reflect your opinions accurately and are understood;
- if possible, make use of the opportunity to ask important questions;
- prepare fully for the interview by reading the information from the school and anticipating likely questions;
- treat internal interviews seriously;
- dress sensibly;
- approach the interview as a positive, learning experience;
- concentrate on highlighting your special skills and interests;
- try to be aware of signals from the panel;
- speak clearly and as naturally as possible;

These guidelines for applicants should provide stimulation for discussion and learning and they should be rewritten where they do not match the reader's experience. It is also necessary for readers to be aware that preparation for promotion means more than learning a few guidelines for being an effective interviewee. It means analysing very carefully the knowledge and skills which are needed for effective performance of the post for which you wish to apply. The required knowledge and skills can be acquired in several ways: for example, attending courses or self-directed staff development in school to gain experience of the activities which form part of the job. A particularly useful preparation is to volunteer for the position of personal assistant or deputy to the position being sought. Another important source of learning is the feedback given to a colleague after an interview. Here is one such review from a headteacher, which raises several interesting points for discussion:

> I hope that you have recovered from the ordeal of the past two days and the disappointment of not being appointed. The following observations are offered as constructive suggestions:
>
> - You are tall and obviously find it difficult to find a suitable seated position, consequently you were shuffling around during the interview. All the panel noticed you cross your foot across your knee, which cannot be comfortable for any length of time. Can I suggest

that you sit firmly in your seat, cross your legs and sit with your hands clasped in your lap until you find out what is comfortable for you?

- I would advise you to relate your answers to the person who has asked the question, because it enables good eye contact to be established. I think some of your discomfort resulted from trying to spray your answers at all the panel.
- Your letter of application was very good, precise and well ordered. Your list of publications shows that you have obviously been a prodigious writer but two of the governors wondered how you had found the time to write so many articles and review so many books. You are obviously well read, but you should not try to impress the panel with the names of books and authors that you have used as it makes them feel out of their depth.
- You are obviously an enthusiastic teacher and you should allow your enthusiasm for the whole school to come through in your answers. You are intelligent and had prepared yourself well for the interview. Your earlier answers were precise and to the point but beware of becoming too anecdotal; towards the end of the hour you were going into such detail that you were straying from the point. As a general rule I advise my staff to talk for three minutes then stop. If the interviewers want to ask further questions they will do so.

My apologies if I appear too critical. I am certain you are a good head of department candidate, and wish you success in the future.

Another important learning exercise is to review one's own interviews. The following questions, can be used as a 'starter':

- Did I talk too much or too little when answering the questions?
- Did I possess sufficient knowledge to answer the questions fully?
- Was I able to answer the questions concisely?
- Were my answers to particular questions given in a logical sequence?
- Did I really want the job?

If the self-review suggests a training need for more skills to answer interview questions, readers should be able to gain specific guidance from *Your Approach to Interview Questions* (Threlfall 1991). He discusses a number of questions frequently asked in middle management selection interviews and suggests ways of answering them to the satisfaction of interviewing panels.

If these guidelines and recommendations enable readers to be successful in appointing staff and in their own applications for promotion they should remind themselves that there is still much work to be done to make a success of the process of professional development. Induction, appraisal and training are also very significant.

INDUCTION

The link between selection and induction is important and if it is weak the benefits of good management practice in the selection process may be lost.

Induction, which should be regarded as a key organisational resource, is the process of introducing the new employee to the organisation and the organisation to the employee. It begins at the appointment stage, with introductions to future colleagues, the provision of information about the organisation and its departments, and information about local environmental facilities such as accommodation. This introductory phase of induction continues before the person starts work. A letter of introduction and welcome is an essential and effective part of the process of familiarisation with the new role. This important letter should be followed up by the minutes of subsequent team meetings which would be relevant to the newcomer's post.

The process continues as soon as the newcomer takes up the appointment. This is necessary for new appointments at all levels of responsibility. It is helpful to set up a formal induction course through which new members of staff learn the policies and systems of the organisation. Humphreys suggests that the best basis from which to start the induction process is the question: what does the newcomer want or need to know (Humphreys 1983)? He recommends that a programme of induction must cover such matters as conditions of employment, departmental information, and general health and safety. He further recommends that the organisers of these programmes remember that newcomers will find it difficult to assimilate a mass of information at one sitting and a suitable time-scale should be devised.

Another contribution to the management of induction in schools which course members have found useful comes from industry and has been published by Bolton Business Ventures Ltd. In their introduction the consultants write that induction:

> will involve training – providing skills and knowledge to help the person during their first few days and weeks. But beyond this it involves managing the whole process of settling the person into the team and the organisation within which they are to work. It is a process which can begin at the recruitment stage – the time when potential recruits may receive their first impressions of, and first information about, the business. And it can stretch well beyond the first few days of employment, as new recruits to many of the complex jobs in business may need several months to become fully functional.
>
> (Bolton Business Ventures Ltd, n.d.: 3)

The consultants discuss in considerable and helpful detail the benefits of sound planning of the first day in the post:

... for a number of reasons the first day of a new recruit's employment requires particular attention. First impressions count for everyone concerned, and it is important that s/he receives a favourable impression of the business and also that existing staff are encouraged to assist new colleagues. New starters are likely to be particularly anxious during their initial period with the business, something which can be alleviated by careful induction planning.

(Bolton Business Ventures Ltd, n.d.: 5)

These recommendations can be compared with two induction programmes for schools devised by course members. The aims and objectives of one programme are followed by the detail of the second (see Figure 6.5).

It is important to acknowledge that effective induction programmes are also needed for part-time and supply staff. Some insight into the needs of the latter can be gained from the following report of an interview conducted by a course member with a supply teacher who had previously been a full-time member of staff.

- Being a supply teacher was in practice starting a new career and quite different from her previous teaching;
- confidence in the classroom had to be re-established;
- the pupils had changed in outlook over six years;
- she had changed;
- clearly, supply teachers, like students, are fair game for pupils who like to test them out;
- a different class each lesson and a fresh set of faces mean that a new relationship, on a temporary basis, has to be forged as frequently as every forty minutes;
- the lack of specialist subject knowledge by supply teachers is not always fully appreciated by staff or pupils;
- the behavioural and ability level of the class needs determination and consideration;
- work set is sometimes woefully inadequate, overdemanding or – if the supply teacher is fortunate – quite suitable.

It is also important to recognise that the effective management of induction should be a whole school concern. To support this suggestion Figure 6.6 shows a letter which is sent out to all newcomers to the school from the chair of the staffroom committee.

The value of successful induction for all newcomers to a school is very similar to the benefits of staff induction identified by Bolton Business Ventures Ltd. They suggest the following positive effects from good management practice in induction:

- It can improve the chance of new recruits quickly becoming effective members of the organisation.

Aim

To set up an induction course for new staff in response to a request for such support at an INSET session.

Objectives

To provide staff with sufficient information to cope with day-to-day routine administration.
To know how to use the teaching resources available.
To know school policy on such matters as discipline, report-writing and relationships with parents.
To be aware of the relationships between the LEA and the school.
To enable staff to understand the school's organisational structure, including staff roles.
To have some information on the area and its facilities in general, and the catchment area in particular.

Components of an induction course

Knowledge	When	How
Meet key people involved with induction	on appointment	personal meeting
Walk around school, pre-reading specified items, school diary, personal timetable, teaching/ tutoring items	pre-service	group, individual, meetings
Fire drill, accident routine, registers (temporary and permanent), pupil absence notes recording procedure, lesson resources, rewards and punishments (merits/detentions), tutor group responsibilities, department record books, letters to parents/routine for communication	initial induction day (penultimate day of summer holiday); final day of holiday for staff, department and house meetings	formal meeting
Meet support staff	first week	informal meeting
Routine for assessing and reporting to parents	first month	formal meeting

© Routledge 1995

Figure 6.5 Two induction programmes

Welcome to new staff

Here is some information which I hope will help you to settle into this school. I begin by outlining the functions of the staffroom committee which exists to serve your interests.

The staffroom committee exists to attend to the welfare of the whole staff from the most recent probationer appointment to the headteacher himself. The committee is itself an elected body with representatives from Upper School, Lower School and non-teaching staff. The representatives this year are as follows . . . .

Representatives serve a two-year voluntary term of office and their roles within the committee are posted on the staffroom noticeboards. The precise functions of the committee cover several areas:

- *To serve as a representative committee* in discussing any matters with the headteacher that staff find would be inappropriately discussed on other committees or with unions. However, such matters may be discussed by the committee if staff are dissatisfied with the representation they have had on those other committees. Any representative may be approached with complaints, ideas or suggestions.
- *To offer a varied programme of social events* throughout the year. It is hoped that you will join fully in any or all of these. If you have suggestions or seek information about these things you should contact the social secretary.
- *To organise the provision of staffroom refreshments* wherever possible.
- *To ensure the general welfare of staff.* This includes the following:
  - to advise and act as 'friend' to any member of staff in need
  - to ensure provision of professional reading materials in staffrooms
  - to contact and arrange gifts for staff suffering from illness or bereavement or those celebrating births
  - to arrange for collections and presentations to be made for leaving staff
  - to collect the agreed staff fund quota of . . .
- *To ensure the tidy upkeep of staffroom noticeboards and the satisfactory management of staffrooms*
- *To act in the general interests of the staff in any way that they may direct within the limits of their capabilities and functions*

The effectiveness of the committee depends almost entirely on the willingness of all staff to involve and support them; please ensure that you take full advantage of the service offered.

Figure 6.6 Letter of welcome to new staff

- It allows mutual expectations concerning the job and employment conditions to be clarified.
- It enables any unnecessary anxieties which new recruits may have to be dispelled.

(Bolton Business Ventures Ltd, n.d.: 3)

The negative consequences of poor induction and the positive effects of good management practice can also be identified in the following report from a course member:

> At my present school there has been no attempt by the Faculty to help integrate me into the secrets of the school's administration, hierarchy and discipline structure. Any advice about personal development has been in response to my own questions and certainly not as part of any systematic school approach. It could perhaps be seen as significant that the atmosphere of the school establishment and the attitude of the staff at my present school are much more negative and even depressed than in my previous school where senior management had introduced an induction programme for all new staff and in a positive – although seemingly unsystematic – way made every attempt to advise and assist staff in their personal and professional prospects. It may well have been due to the individuals involved, the more attractive location of the school and the nature of the catchment area, or a whole range of other variables, but certainly the belief in a reasonably caring and supportive system for the staff was recognisable and important.

The importance of sound induction management following on from an effective selection process has been strongly demonstrated by the recommendations and reports in the previous pages. But professional development makes continuous demands on management and it does not end with successful induction. The next vital task of the effective management of human resources is appraisal, which is discussed in the next chapter.

Chapter 7

Continuing professional development: appraisal and training

Course members trying to achieve the management tasks of appraisal and training have identified the following training needs:

* learning how to develop personal confidence with a view to promotion;
* learning how to move forward professionally;
* learning how to enhance personal performance in school.

APPRAISAL

It is important for readers to be aware that the term 'appraisal' is used in two different ways and they should be clear about which meaning is being used in discussions of the planning and implementation of appraisal projects. Poster and Poster name two concepts: performance appraisal and staff development review (Poster and Poster 1993: 1). Performance appraisal is concerned with setting achievable goals and giving feedback to staff on their work performance which identifies their training needs and encourages better performance, so that the objectives of the organisation can be achieved. Staff development reviews are concerned with the identification of teachers' professional development needs and the training opportunities to satisfy these needs, so that teachers can improve their performance in present and future work roles.

Performance appraisal

Performance appraisal provides valuable opportunities for satisfying crucial organisational needs. These are:

* assessment of past and present performance and prediction of future contributions from each member of staff;
* an overview of current and potential skills, resources and capabilities available for human resource management in the organisation to meet present and future challenges;
* identification of training needs.

This form of appraisal is receiving strong encouragement from those movements which are trying to give consumers a greater say in the delivery of many different services, such as education, transport and health. One observer of the expansion has reported:

> Whether it is Citizen's Charter or Passenger's Charter, school examin-ation league tables or health service waiting lists, the result is the same. Service delivery is to be monitored as never before, as information is seen as the key to developing motivation and customer satisfaction.
>
> Some form of personal assessment scheme or 'individual perform-ance review' is an essential item in the tool bag of the modern public sector personnel manager. It is accompanied by the parallel desire to reward staff on the basis of their performance: payment by results rather than the old image of being paid for turning up for work. The principles are being applied widely, in all areas of public service from Whitehall civil servants and local authority staff to hospital trusts and British Rail managers.
>
> (Whitfield 1992: 31)

The possibility that appraisal in the managerial style, relying heavily on targets, performance indicators and incentives, might become part of the National Framework has aroused powerful criticism on several grounds:

> The rapidity of change may well invalidate or modify the goals that managers have set; lower echelon staff have little control over the factors that affect goal achievement and therefore little motivation to take responsibility; and, particularly true of education, despite the present emphasis on the identification of performance criteria, there are large areas in which specific targets cannot be identified and which may be undervalued in any review of this kind.
>
> (Poster and Poster 1993: 10)

Staff development review

Other critics have argued that performance appraisal results in an ex-clusive focus on accountability, cost cutting, judgemental reactions and critical feedback, rather than the enhancement of teachers' feelings of self-esteem, confidence and motivation which the staff development model of accountability predicts might follow from the introduction of appraisal. The benefits of this approach to appraisal include satisfying important teachers' needs such as knowing what is expected of them, having feed-back about how their work is evaluated, being able to discuss their strengths and weaknesses objectively and constructively, feeling valued by receiving recognition for effort as well as for achievement, being aware of personal and professional growth, and identification of training needs.

By reinforcing teachers' feelings of being valued for their contribution at work, Blackburn has also noted the benefits which the developmental model of appraisal can bring:

> Too often in schools the esteem in which teachers' work is held is left unspoken. To feel valued for the work that has been done motivates teachers to make future effort. More precisely there is the opportunity to recall the things teachers have specifically undertaken in the last year which, apart from having been beneficial to the pupils and the departmental team, have served to give the teachers areas of work through which they have found some sense of fulfilment.
>
> (Blackburn 1986: 51)

The benefits and negative feelings which staff could experience from appraisal are closely related to the management and culture of the school in which they work. Duffy has put this point very strongly: 'Appraisal brings huge benefits in school when teachers perceive that it is they who own the process and where the context is collegial' (Duffy 1990: 37). He goes on to argue that only a few schools nationally have developed such a culture of participative management styles as to warrant the term 'collegial'. Fortunately for those staff who wish to enjoy some of the advantages of the developmental model of appraisal, it is possible to see the introduction of appraisal in school leading to a greater degree of involvement in decision making. These issues are discussed in a report by one of my course members (Figure 7.1).

This report presents a clear perspective of the major tasks and problems associated with appraisal. To meet these successfully requires a high level of managerial competence and the training to achieve it. Other reports strongly support this conclusion.

Bradley *et al.* suggest that for some teachers an accurate, balanced self-review might be difficult because they find it easier to be self-critical than to be positive about their strengths (Bradley *et al.* 1989). Grice and Hanke have warned against some of the problems which can arise in the classroom observation of a teacher. They note that an appraiser in the classroom may disturb patterns of relationships between teacher and pupil and between pupils themselves: 'An observer however skilful will be an alien to the regular pattern of classroom relationships and could affect the normal running of classroom events' (Grice and Hanke 1990: 42). They argue that any observation, or even a number of observations, may be an unrepresentative sampling of teacher and pupil behaviour. They refer to one of the 'more sinister' aspects of teacher appraisal which is revealed in the DES publication *Better Schools*:

> Appraisal should lead to the most promising and effective teachers being identified for timely promotion, with those encountering

The staff of my school were introduced to appraisal through an INSET day led by a management consultant. At the start of the day the staff were asked to outline their hopes and fears for the system on the basis of their existing knowledge of appraisal. These are summarised below:

Staff's initial hopes for and fears of appraisal

Hopes

- increased knowledge of colleagues and their work;
- professional development, positive feedback on teaching techniques;
- recognition of teaching skills of the classroom practitioner;
- that the school's appraisal scheme should evolve from what we already do;
- that the school development plan should equal the total of appraisal targets.

Fears

- time away from classes;
- lack of consistency;
- will appraisers have the necessary interpersonal skills?;
- will the appraisee necessarily agree with the senior management team's opinion of the best person to do the appraising?;
- possible manipulation of staff into 'other duties';
- the eventual linking of appraisal to performance-related pay.

The appraisal process

The management consultant presented the specified requirements of the appraisal process as laid down in the DES Regulations (DES 1991).

The deputy head reported that the appraisal system consists of the following phases:

- the initial meeting;
- self-appraisal (optional);
- classroom/task observation;
- collection of other data (optional);
- the appraisal discussion;
- the appraisal statement;
- follow-up discussions and professional development activities;
- the review meeting.

This to take place over a two-year cycle.

The deputy head emphasised that the initial meeting forms the scene-setting for the whole process. Central, as a point of reference, is the job description. Again, the link with the rest of the staff development chain should be made clear here. The job description needs to be clearly stated during the selection process and any problems ironed out during induction. If this is undertaken properly then the use of the job description during appraisal makes great sense; if the contents of the job description are, however, unclear then the appraisal system may fall down at the first hurdle. The senior management team has recently issued staff with new, clearly stated job descriptions and therefore feels confident that it *can* be used as the key document for appraisal. The senior management team, in order to encourage a degree of self-appraisal, also proposes a self-appraisal form is given to every member of staff in good time before the initial meeting. It is generally accepted that unless the appraisee is prepared to spend some time before the appraisal interview systematically reflecting upon work done in the past year and thinking through his/her aspirations and plans for the future, there is a risk that he/she will not be able to contribute to any dialogue. [The form is set out in Figure 7.2.]

It appears that the senior management team is prepared to make time available and be sufficiently prepared to make the initial phase of appraisal run smoothly. The senior management team, perhaps sensitive to criticism that the first INSET day had not really laid to rest many of the fears of the staff, followed up the initial training by organising another full day INSET for staff two terms later. The stated aim of the day was to enable staff to become familiar with the process and to allay any existing fears by showing in detail how, through role play exercises and video extracts, the individual stages would be undertaken. The video extract, introduced by the deputy head, sought to reassure staff about what is potentially the most feared aspect of appraisal, that of classroom observation. Staff were carefully guided through the fundamentals of classroom observation. Although a serious matter, this was undertaken in such a way as to set staff deliberately at ease and the deputy head, by his sympathetic approach, helped greatly to deflect much of the expected criticism.

Anxieties were expressed, however, that appraisers' perceptions of a 'good' lesson may differ radically. Most of the complaints that staff expressed related to the possible choice of appraiser. Certainly it would seem that not all those with responsibilities for appraising were felt by many potential appraisees to be best qualified for the job. Many would prefer to be appraised by someone of equal status to their own line manager, another head of department for example. The reasons for this were varied, but the general feeling was that it may prove to be difficult to speak frankly, and perhaps criticise directly, a head of department and then have to work closely with that person the next day. The view was rejected categorically by senior management, who obviously felt that if such strong feelings existed the matter should have been raised sooner. It is clearly expected, therefore, that the line manager will perform the duty.

Once complete, the classroom observation is followed by the appraisal interview. The DES regulations summarise the list of topics for discussion as:

- further consideration of the job description if necessary;
- a review of the teacher's work since the last appraisal;
- discussion of professional development needs;
- discussion of career development;
- discussion of the teacher's role in and contribution to school management and policies, and identification of any constraints which the school places on the teacher;

- identification of targets for future action and development;
- clarification of points to be involved in the appraisal statement.

It is interesting to note that the word 'development' appears three times here. However, teachers expressed concern that resources may not be made available for such development to take place effectively.

Interviews I conducted with staff after the second training day showed that a lack of resources for training and development remains a big point of contention for staff. Without those resources being made available, many find it difficult to see how the aim of developing professionalism can possibly be achieved. Without the essential link between appraisal and training being fully funded and supported, more and more teachers may come to regard the accountability aspect of appraisal as more important than the developmental aspect.

© Routledge 1995

Figure 7.1 Examples of different forms of appraisal

professional difficulties being promptly identified for appropriate counselling, guidance and support, and where such assistance does not restore performance to a satisfactory level with the teacher concerned being recommended for retirement or dismissal.

(DES 1985: para. 180)

Grice and Hanke believe that this approach would not inspire the confidence or the trust which are so essential for the successful use of staff appraisal. But on the positive side, there are also reports which suggest guidelines for tackling these difficulties. Hancock and Settle have attempted to provide a practical guide to help teachers review their own performance at work. They have presented exercises, activity sheets and questions to facilitate this task (Hancock and Settle 1992).

Warwick has offered guidelines for good practice for review interviews, which should be: 'regular, informal, frank, two-way, individual, confidential, positive, constructive, productive and supportive' (Warwick 1983).

Successful interviews are those thoroughly prepared by both the interviewer and the interviewee. They begin well, continue well and end well. They begin, as I have emphasised, with selection interviewing, with the interviewer putting the interviewee at ease and establishing rapport. The right approach again, in addition to the interpersonal interaction, is to show consideration by careful attention to the administrative details and by providing a physical setting which is free from distraction and interruption.

This good beginning can be continued by keeping to the agenda: the job description, the targets set at the previous review meeting, achievements and failures and the reasons for them, the agreement of future objectives and training if appropriate.

As part of the annual cycle of teacher performance appraisal you can have a discussion with your headteacher/appraiser about your work during this academic year and your work plan for the coming year. The purpose of this process is to identify needs for the professional growth of all teachers and to promote teacher effectiveness by endeavouring to meet these needs wherever possible.

You may find it helpful to prepare yourself by answering these questions in advance of the interview although you are not required to make the completed form available to your appraiser if you prefer not to do so.

• Write down what you think are the main tasks and responsibilities of your current post.

• During the past academic year, what parts of your job have given you greatest satisfaction?
• How could these be used to best advantage?

• What parts of your job have given you least satisfaction?
• Is there something that could be done to overcome this?

• Were there any problems or difficulties which prevented you from achieving something you intended or hoped to do?
• Are they still a cause for concern?
• If so, could they be eliminated?

• To help improve your performance in your job, what changes in the school organisation would be beneficial?

• What additional things might be done by your headteacher?
• Your head of department?
• You?
• Anyone else?

• What do you think should be your main target(s)/goals for next year?

• How would you like to see your career developing?

© Routledge 1995

Figure 7.2 Example of a self-appraisal/interview preparation form

A good interview ends well. Both interviewer and interviewee are satisfied that:

• all aspects of the staff member's work have been discussed;
• an overall evaluation has been agreed;
• objectives/targets have been agreed for the next review period;
• training and other resources where necessary have been offered to achieve these goals.

The task of data collection from sources of information other than interviews can be facilitated by using feedback from colleagues.

A head of department who was also a member of one of my courses has provided an example from his school of the benefits of appraisal by one's peers:

> During the last academic year in the writer's school, a group of teachers, from a wide range of subjects, formed a self-support group. Their aim was to assist each other in the development of classroom skills. Since the classroom is a major source of stressful situations, this seemed a commendable scheme in that it was initiated by themselves and not by senior management. The group members attended each other's lessons as observers and, using a previously drawn-up format for classroom teaching, commented constructively on each other's methods and development over the course of the year. Members of the group commented on the following benefits they felt they had received:
>
> - identifying skills in others absent in themselves;
> - becoming aware of pressures faced by teachers in other subjects;
> - becoming aware of the change in pupils' attitudes with subject;
> - being able to offer and accept advice from colleagues in a non-critical atmosphere;
> - having a feeling that others were interested in your work;
> - the development of respect, confidence and trust in each other's views and feeling related to their school work.

This type of appraisal had the unexpected benefit of helping with stress management. But in this head of department's school not all his colleagues became involved in this type of appraisal. Other evaluation programmes have used a whole school approach, involving all members of staff. One of these developments has been carefully documented by the initiator of the review programme, Peter Thompson, former head of Wheatcroft School, Scarborough. He and the staff wrote a brief report of their work after it had been in operation for four years. He argues that a whole-school approach to appraisal should be 'school initiated and self-generating' (Thompson 1987). For the procedure to be effective 'the whole staff will need to be involved'. The areas of the school for review by staff should be decided upon by staff from the following list: aims, building and general environment, children, curriculum, ethos, finance and resources, governors, headteacher, home, school and community, liaison, non-teaching staff, organisation, post-holders, staff development, teacher appraisal. Each of these areas was discussed in turn by using the Spring term for discussion and the Summer and Autumn terms to implement all the recommendations. Two half-hour sessions during the week whilst the head took the school for assembly/hymn practice and a further hour after school each week were used for discussions, which were focused by having no more than five statements for each area. For example:

Headteacher
- The headteacher should visit each class every day and speak to members of staff individually.
- The headteacher should spend part of each day teaching.
- The headteacher should take steps to ensure that he shows an active interest in the professional development, advancement and personal welfare of staff.
- Parents should feel at ease when they visit the school.

But for teacher appraisal the framework for the staff discussions was changed. Instead of the statements, a brief policy paper was prepared which included the following recommendations:

- Teacher appraisal should be seen as an extension of the school self-evaluation process. Teaching staff with the experience of discussing areas within the school will approach appraisal with less apprehension.
- If it is seen to be a means of improving the quality of education, through the development and improvement of teacher skills, then it has every chance of being successful.
- Until headteachers are appraised, the appraisal of teaching staff will not be accepted.
- Before appraisal can take place, all teaching staff will require clearly defined job descriptions.
- Areas of appraisal will, in the main, fall into two categories: the interview and classroom observation, and, in the case of the headteacher, observation of his duties over an agreed period.

Four years after its inauguration the School Self-Evaluation Project had covered 10 of the original 15 areas for review. It was anticipated that the remaining areas would be completed within the next 18 months. At the four-year stage the overall conclusion of the staff was:

> To sum up, we all feel that it has been a helpful and worthwhile exercise. We have learned more about ourselves and our colleagues and we feel we have been able to clarify a common philosophy for the school to work in. We are well aware there are, and will be, areas of weakness where discussion is needed in relation to personalities, but surely to be able to discuss one's professional aims and objectives with one's colleagues in a rational manner is part of our development as professional teachers.
>
> (Thompson 1987: 27)

These positive reports of good management practice to achieve the tasks and reduce the difficulties of implementing appraisal policies and procedures suggest the importance of putting appraisal in the context of a school's integrated staff development policy. I have already suggested that selection should dovetail with induction, which should lead to appraisal by means of the review interview in the induction programme. And training objectives for teaching and support staff should be focused by appraisal.

Good opportunities are thereby provided for the satisfaction of important staff needs. These include:

- knowing what is expected of them;
- receiving feedback about their work;
- being able to discuss their difficulties objectively and constructively;
- feeling valued by receiving recognition for effort as well as achievement;
- being aware of personal and professional growth.

TRAINING

It is a good organisational resource to link the review or appraisal system to in-service training provision, so that appropriate opportunities are offered for continuing staff development. One secondary school headteacher reviewing the introduction of appraisal in a report to staff concluded:

We have assembled a list of INSET needs and are beginning to implement them. A need has emerged for training aspiring and existing heads of department in the skills of middle management in schools. A course is being planned for next term.

But this headteacher also rightly emphasised that INSET is just one part of staff development in the school. Others included in his report were:

Regular interviews with the head about matters of professional development, opportunities to exchange posts within the school, involvement with a range of new curriculum and other initiatives, a rolling programme of departmental evaluation undertaken by the head, hopefully a positive ethos in the school which encourages all staff to build on our strengths and to identify and rectify our weaknesses.

A secondary head of year prepared a review of some of the training opportunities she believed to be necessary to achieve the objectives of a staff development programme. She recommended that information, advice and support must be readily available to staff through individual, team and whole school approaches. These included:

- the availability of a professional tutor for all members of staff to discuss issues such as the development of classroom management and

control skills, opportunities to observe colleagues or visit other schools, discussion of INSET and career opportunities, and help with letters of application and interview techniques;
- the accessibility of information relating to courses, secondments, current educational issues and training opportunities;
- an open invitation to join working parties related to school policies;
- faculty in-service training, with head of faculty taking the responsibility for developing individual teachers' in-service needs;
- year team in-service training, where year heads encourage the development of the team's pastoral skills;
- management in-service training for heads of curriculum/year/faculty and senior managers;
- whole school in-service training, including staff meetings and conferences.

Important recommendations for the continuing professional development of support staff were made by the technicians and administrative staff of the Sixth Form college as part of the college INSET programme for which I was the management consultant.

The following recommendations were made by the technicians:

- time should be available for technicians to meet;
- there should be opportunities for technicians and support staff to give presentations;
- needs should be anticipated by careful pre-planning;
- there should be an opportunity to attend staff meetings;
- there should be a development programme for support staff;
- there should be a recognition of personal time/space by others;
- there should be more consultative time;
- there should be more opportunities for consultation with members of the executive.

The following recommendations were made by the administrative staff:

- non-teaching staff should have equal status with teaching staff;
- staff meetings should be attended by all categories of staff;
- there should be better liaison between staff;
- the office should give a presentation of available services; it was felt that sometimes we were abused rather than used;
- teaching staff should recognise the space and time belonging to administrative staff;
- administrative deadlines should be met;
- there should be a development plan for support staff;
- training should be given in the new technology and assertiveness;
- there should be INSET for support staff.

Shropshire Education Department invited a writing team of primary headteachers and advisers to compile a booklet on 'Management Development in Primary Schools'. They produced, in January 1993, a brief, thorough and innovative report which merits attention and discussion. The team emphasised the importance of a 'clear and positive staff development policy which offers opportunities for professional growth' (Shropshire Education Department 1993: 3). An important contribution to growth consists of the management skills which all staff members need to use – 'each has therefore an entitlement to management training' (ibid.).

The opportunities for developing these skills suggested by the writing team can be found in the school, around the school and beyond the school. Different 'menus' of activities for teachers at the four main levels of incentive allowance holder, curriculum leader, deputy headteacher and headteacher in the primary phase are recommended, depending on whether they are in the induction, consolidation or further development phases of their appointment. An example of the menus for an incentive allowance holder is given in Table 7.1.

Table 7.1 Opportunities for developing management skills

Incentive allowance holder	In the school	Around the school	Beyond the school
Induction	Identifying priorities and an agenda for action; negotiating and agreeing this with the team and with senior staff	Discussing the role with other coordinators in the school	Attending INSET on curricular development and the managerial role of curriculum coordinators
Consolidation	Planning and leading team meetings; arranging the agenda and minutes; writing and presenting papers for discussion	Sharing the day-to-day management of the school	Conducting action research in own school, possibly using distance learning materials
Further development	Exchanging tasks with a peer with different responsibilities	Shadowing a colleague to broaden management experience	Seeking a short industrial placement through the Teacher Placement Scheme

The writing team in their introduction made a very important statement which all readers should carefully consider:

> It is a menu to dip into and choose from, not a recipe of required ingredients. The distinctions are certainly not hard and fast and the selection of activities will depend upon personal wishes and needs and upon the size and circumstances of individual schools. By having their own copies, teachers can select, negotiate and undertake tasks which are appropriate and build up a portfolio of management experience.
>
> (Shropshire Education Department 1993: 3)

The guidelines for self-directed management development programmes at the four levels of incentive allowance holder, curriculum leader, deputy headteacher and headteacher could be useful for appraisal, in the identification of training needs and in keeping a cumulative record of widening managerial experience which could be used as part of job applications.

Yet it is necessary to note the limitations of the Shropshire booklet. There is no discussion of listening, decision making or delegating. The items in the booklet are concerned with what to do rather than how to do it. There is also no reference to tasks and skills which are common to all four levels of post, such as the management of time, change and stress.

I want to conclude this chapter by briefly reporting two of the interesting innovations in training which are now available for readers. One of these is distance learning. The advantages claimed for this approach to management development include:

- flexibility in learning times and places for hard-pressed school staff;
- direct support to school, focused action, learning through collaborative project work, etc.;
- effective and efficient use of scarce specialist expertise;
- bringing management development closer to the school and helping to make it more widely available at a realistic cost.

(Glatter 1993: 126)

Another innovative approach is the use of interactive videos. These can play an important part in approaches to management development which emphasise a greater use of training rather than external courses. According to a paper by Bowring-Carr, interactive video is a powerful medium for learning because it 'combines the advantages of conventional video with the power and flexibility of the computer' (Bowring-Carr 1993: 131).

As with distance learning, training can take place at times and locations which are convenient to both the individual and the school as a whole. Bowring-Carr describes in the following paragraph some of the major advantages of this approach:

Interactive video provides, on laserdisc, a wealth of filmed material of high quality, either long scenes, such as interviews or staff meetings, or very short scenes, each highlighting a particular problem or situation that can occur in any school. The scene can be found precisely and quickly through the use of frame numbers, as can any frame within the scene. The scene can be stopped at any point, for discussion and analysis, and the picture can be held on-screen indefinitely without deterioration. At the end of the scene, the computer-generated text can set a number of discussion points, ask questions, sum up the cumulative responses of the user, and refer the user to further reading.

(Bowring-Carr 1993: 132)

In the company where I am an employee development and training consultant, staff from every level of responsibility, from managing director to apprentice, have responded very positively to the opportunities to use interactive videos for personal and professional development in the company's Open Learning Centre. The ease of access and the self-directing and self-pacing aspects of these learning opportunities are powerful motivators. These developments have extended quite significantly the range of possibilities for continuing professional development.

Some teachers find it useful to have some assistance in order to gain optimum benefit from the wider range of choices now available. It was reported in Chapter 1 that members of my courses are advised to seek a mentor in their school who will help them to establish and maintain a bridge between school and university course. The mentor will discuss the course working resources and suggest additional sources of learning. In some schools and industries mentors have a wider role, which includes specific skills, coaching and counselling, to facilitate realistic career goals and choices. They will have an important contribution to make to school-based teacher training programmes. The relationship between the mentor and his apprentice is a unique one and ground rules made by both parties for their cooperation are necessary. Finn has suggested the following framework:

- a mentoring contract to set down the rules of the relationship;
- clear objectives, which will change as the relationship develops;
- development tasks which will support the development of the protegé in the areas agreed. These could be in the form of work assignments, having the opportunity to sit next to an appropriate 'Nellie', or distance learning, for example;
- monitoring the mentoring relationship to see that the contract is being carried out to the satisfaction of both parties; and
- an occasional review to check the health of the relationship.

(Finn 1993: 153)

But for new learning opportunities to be used effectively, whether they be on-site or off-site, both mentor and apprentice have a crucial task to accomplish and that is the management of time. This is the focus of our next chapter.

Chapter 8

Effective time management

The effective management of time is a major concern for teachers joining my management courses and some of their objectives are:

- as a head of department to find the best way of organising time/duties/ resources of permanent and part-time staff;
- the time management of self and others;
- to fit the unexpected into a tight schedule;
- to know how and to whom to say 'No';
- to manage our time better and more productively;
- time management to reduce stress and become more effective.

This chapter aims to help readers learn and practise the necessary skills to achieve these objectives. The time pressures reported by teaching and support staff are identified. These include:

- having to do three things at once;
- keeping to deadlines that appear impossible;
- unnecessary paperwork.

Self-induced time pressures include:

- procrastination;
- poor personal planning;
- bad filing systems.

Time-management strategies to reduce these pressures can bring considerable benefits, such as clearer thinking, better forward planning and better quality work. Strategies which are recommended include identifying the main source of time loss and blocking up the holes! These may be from interruptions or from poorly managed meetings, which I call 'time theft'. Suggestions are given for preparing and implementing a time-managed contract with a partner.

Time management is an essential skill at all levels of experience and responsibility. It is an individual, team and whole school requirement for effective work performance. For many colleagues it appears to be a difficult skill to learn and to practise; for some it seems to be one in which it is almost impossible for them to become proficient! These relatively few members cause a disproportionate number of difficulties for others because of late or missed deadlines, rushed and poor preparation, omissions and the theft of colleagues' time.

For those colleagues who experience considerable and continuing difficulties, being given a list of exhortations is rarely helpful. It can also be counter-productive, as teachers feel let down as the old problems reappear. My approach is to recommend that readers have a learning partner to share a four-part contract for improving their performance as time managers.

IMPROVING PERSONAL TIME MANAGEMENT – THE CONTRACT

Readers working with a partner should agree at the outset on the terms of their contract, which could include the following suggestions.

- Each person's contract should include details related to each of the four parts to make it successful, which means identifying the anticipated benefits, the external and self-imposed time pressures, the training needs and the skills to satisfy the needs, and should include regular reviews of progress.
- Each contract should be dated and signed by both parties and the agreed termination date should be included.
- Contact should be made by the partners at the beginning of each week to share their plans for the week and their specific targets for practice and improvement.
- There should be brief weekly reviews to share and celebrate success and to offer support for continuing difficulties.

1 Agreeing on benefits to be gained

The first part of the contract is to agree on the benefits to be gained from this programme, which should continue for a limited period. At the end of the contract the partners should review their progress. Readers may now want to identify the benefits to be expected from their improved time-management skills. When they have completed their lists they could compare them with the following ten benefits of successful time management suggested by an experienced head of department:

- more effective stress management;
- clearer thinking;
- better forward planning;
- more time available for more important tasks;

- better personal relationships;
- better use of information;
- greater self-confidence and credibility;
- better quality of work;
- more work done;
- improvement of career prospects.

Readers will probably have added further benefits to this list. It is also likely that more time, energy, concentration and patience will be available for three important concerns:

- taking full advantage of the learning opportunities for continuing professional development, as discussed in the previous chapter;
- the teacher's family and friends;
- the teacher's hobbies and other activities which provide valuable alternative lifestyles to work.

2 Identification of time pressures

The second part of the contract is the identification of time pressures on the partners at work. Readers should make their own list before using the following list, which was compiled by the staff of the Sixth Form college referred to in the last chapter as part of their INSET programme:

- meeting a number of deadlines simultaneously;
- insufficient time for routine tasks or examining new developments;
- not enough time to prepare lessons properly;
- not having enough time to file things carefully;
- having to use family time to fit it all in;
- general overload of paperwork and sometimes unnecessary meetings diverting attention away from lesson preparation and marking;
- spending staff training days on topics which should not take first priority over actual training, such as bringing teachers up to date with new methods and new equipment;
- increased demand on my time due to LMS and therefore not being able to do my job to my satisfaction.

If one or both of the partners in the contract is a member of the support staff, he/she should compare his/her time pressures with those identified by the administrative staff during the same college INSET day:

> The discussion started with some frank comments on how the office staff frequently felt that they were regarded as second class citizens as far as the staffing of the college was concerned. It was felt that we were expected to do too many jobs at the same time. We are expected to keep all equipment running smoothly, whether we use it or not; we are

expected to stop what we are doing to attend to someone's needs even though we are undertaking (mostly without training) tasks for LMS.

The office staff see themselves as an integral part of the college and consider that they have three main roles:

As a working department,
As a support to the rest of the staff,
As the first contact point in the college, responsible for receiving visitors and projecting a good image.

They believe that they have a role to play in the time management of the teaching staff. It was generally considered that, although the office staff are very aware of the changes which are taking place in the teaching profession, it was doubtful whether the teaching profession was aware of all the changes which administrative staff are having to take on board.

(Dunham 1992: 182)

This analysis of time pressures is strongly supported in an article by Michael Warrington, who is headteacher of the Radcliffe School in Oldham. His main conclusions are that:

The volume of administrative work in schools has increased enormously in recent years. LMS itself has added a whole new layer of tasks. Under-provision in the school office creates unacceptable pressures on overworked support staff. It may also result in poor impressions being conveyed to visitors, who may alight on apparent chaos when they arrive for an appointment. No school can afford to have a poor reputation in this or any other area nowadays.

The support staff in many schools would be hard pressed to write down their job descriptions. Their jobs have grown like Topsy, they have been thoroughly taken advantage of and been asked to do far more than their inadequate pay merits. Many school offices are like Clapham Junction; a lot of traffic passes through them and some of it could be re-routed elsewhere to relieve congestion. As in almost every other area of education, there has been a great expansion in the amount of work that support staff are asked to do. They cannot work efficiently with the stream of unwarranted interruptions, nor with staff coming in to borrow the stapler or to exchange gossip.

(Warrington 1993: 136–41)

Readers may find that support staff in their school are experiencing similar pressures. It would be good management practice, as a first step towards reducing them, for these pressures to be identified, so that support staff can be effective in their three roles of administration, logistical support for teaching colleagues and public relations.

Before considering recommendations for reducing time pressures it is necessary to look at another significant source of time-management problems. These are self-induced and if readers suffer from them they will recognise them in the following list:

- being indecisive;
- switching priorities;
- lack of objectives;
- personal disorganisation;
- 'butterflying' from job to job;
- plunging into tasks without planning;
- lack of discipline;
- being involved in too many things;
- procrastinating;
- leaving the difficult tasks 'until later';
- feeling indispensable;
- attempting to do too much at one time;
- constantly misjudging the time tasks take;
- poor or non-existent filing systems;
- being unable to say no.

There are 15 items in this list, which can be used as a checklist by the contract partners to gain an understanding of where to begin the third part of the contract.

3 Identifying time problems and training needs

In this third part the partners should indicate the items on the list which represent their time problems and their training needs.

4 Selecting skills to be practised and reviewed

The fourth and last part of the contract is to select a small number of skills to be practised and reviewed. The practice can be based on the framework proposed by John Adair in his book *Effective Leadership*:

- Record where your time goes.
- Plan ahead. Plan in respect of priorities and deadlines.
- Make the most of your best time.
- Avoid clutter. Sort papers into categories according to action priorities.
- Generate as little paper as possible yourself.
- Do it now.
- Learn to say 'No'. Do not let others misappropriate your time.
- Decline tactfully but firmly to avoid over-commitment.

(Adair 1983: 155)

This contract is for the improvement of personal time-management skills. But readers will know from their own experience that many time problems for teaching and support staff are caused by poor management practice. So it is necessary to consider how to improve organisational time-management skills as well as those that are personal.

IMPROVING ORGANISATIONAL TIME MANAGEMENT

The main difficulties have been revealed as:

- simultaneous deadlines and other pressures;
- poorly managed meetings;
- too much time spent on what staff consider to be irrelevant activities.

As a result of the INSET programme in the Sixth Form college, decisions were taken and implemented by the senior management team to improve the management structure and practice in the college. The INSET co-ordinator in a six-month review of progress sent me a report from which the following details have been extracted:

- office staff and technicians have access to all meetings in college;
- a non-teaching and teaching staff support group was started. It meets weekly. It acts as a focus for the identification of new pressures on staff;
- the executive has tried very hard to respond to the demands from the support group;
- a year plan, providing information about important dates, deadlines and activities, has been placed on a wall in the staffroom;
- the management structure in the college has been redrafted to clarify all roles and areas of responsibility, including the kitchen staff.

This review suggests that it is possible, after the analysis of training needs in an INSET programme, to plan, prepare and produce whole-school policies and procedures aimed at the improvement of organisational time management. When this whole school approach is combined with personal contracts, a powerful strategy has been set in operation for time-management skills to develop.

The next chapter considers whether or not the same positive conclusion can be made for the effective development of the skills of change management.

Chapter 9

The skills of change management

The objectives of course members related to effective change management include:

- learning how to keep up with the changes;
- learning how to work to somebody else's agenda;
- learning how to manage change;
- learning how to implement policy changes.

In this chapter evidence of the successful management of change is presented and guidelines for effective change management are recommended. These include the proposal that the curricular and organisational initiatives stemming from the Education Reform Act 1988 and subsequent legislation can have positive as well as negative aspects, such as more clearly defined expectations and roles and more feedback for staff. The guidelines also contain proposals to restrict the possible negative impact of these changes. These include:

- restrict any other changes that are not related to educational reform legislation to the absolute minimum;
- support your colleagues (including the senior management team and middle management) if they need it, and let them support you if you need it;
- provide help to colleagues so they can face up to change.

Specific changes are discussed to consider how they can be managed well. They include marketing initiatives.

SKILLS USED BY TEACHERS MANAGING CHANGE EFFECTIVELY

Evidence of the skills used by teachers who have been successful in managing external and internal initiatives has been presented in a report for the Department for Education by Bolam *et al.* Their research project into the effective management of schools involved 57 schools, including primary, middle and secondary, and a Sixth Form college, which had volunteered to take part. The results and conclusions were derived from postal questionnaires and from interviews with members of staff in 12 of the schools. The focus of the research was to find out how staff in these schools had effectively managed what the authors of the report describe as:

> Unprecedented change in education with schools and LEAs facing multiple large-scale innovations which have to be implemented in a short time-scale. These changes were predominantly national external initiatives but internal changes such as the arrival of a new head and various attempts at restructuring were also affecting schools in the sample.
>
> (Bolam *et al.* 1993: 84)

The main factors identified by staff in their successful adaptation to different policies, practices and people include:

- The headteacher had allocated financial and other resources to them.
- The collegial management styles of the headteacher and the senior management team had facilitated the development of collaborative whole school structures, such as year teams, and ways of working for planning, consultation and decision making.
- The headteacher, senior management teams and other senior staff had helped to reduce staff stress by developing teamwork and by showing concern and consideration for the effects of innovation on staff and reassuring them about their capabilities, skills and expertise.

> (Bolam *et al.* 1993: 98)

But staff in the survey also reported that they had managed some initiatives more effectively than others. Most of them felt that their school was making effective use of the National Curriculum. The use of professional training days was regarded more positively by primary staff than by secondary staff, while the use of local management of schools was perceived more positively by secondary staff.

In exploring the contributions of all levels of management to the change process in school it is helpful to consider the work of consultants from industry. One of those whose analysis and recommendations are relevant to the vital roles of middle management in facilitating both external and internal innovations is Roger Plant. He is a freelance consultant specialising in change management and team development. He was formerly a Director at Ashridge Management College. In the introduction to his book *Managing Change*, Plant refers to:

> The Westland affair and the protracted dispute between the teachers and the government, which illustrated par excellence how not to handle change and influence events successfully. The rights and wrongs of the

conflicts themselves are not important to our purpose here. What they both demonstrate powerfully are the dire and expensive consequences of not paying sufficient attention to the ways and means of implementing change. The key factor in both situations has become the way in which the people involved *feel* they have been treated.

(Plant 1987: 12)

UNDERSTANDING RESISTANCE TO CHANGE

Plant's work in helping individuals and organisations face up to change starts with the assumption that 'resistance to change is a natural phenomenon. It does not come from sheer cussedness, it needs to be recognised, understood and managed. This is true of organisation and systems as well as of individuals' (Plant 1987: 29). He lists the most frequent sources of resistance to change as:

* fear of the unknown;
* lack of information;
* misinformation;
* historical factors;
* threat to core skills and competence;
* threat to status;
* threat to power base;
* no perceived benefits;
* low trust organisational climate;
* poor relationships;
* fear of failure;
* fear of looking stupid;
* reluctance to experiment;
* custom bound;
* reluctance to let go;
* strong peer group norms.

(Plant 1987: 18)

Plant suggests that these cases are often indicated by some of the following signs of resistance, which may be expressed by staff in meetings, staffroom conversations and discussions between individual members of staff and their middle and senior management. Readers will probably be familiar with some of those included in the following list. They might even have used some of them themselves:

'We tried that years ago and it didn't work.'
'A lot of change is just for the sake of change.'
'If only I had time.'
'I have never stood in the way of progress, but . . . '

'This requires extensive and thorough analysis.'

(Plant 1987: 17)

Readers may also like to add other statements indicating resistance to change which they are experiencing. They may also be familiar with such behavioural and emotional signs of resistance as anger, lack of cooperation, lack of effort, lack of involvement, unwillingness to attend meetings, cynicism, looking for other jobs and other careers outside teaching, early retirement, withdrawal of the department from the school's activities.

Three members of my courses have reported their personal experience of these reactions in some detail. A head of department wrote:

> During this academic year we have been faced with tremendous reorganisation plans in an attempt to implement the National Curriculum and keep the range of subjects, particularly classics, available to pupils. Heads of departments, for the first time, have found themselves fighting for their subjects, trying to deal with overmanning in certain departments, having to devise new courses and find new resources. Their role has completely changed. In addition they have also had to deal with their department's anxiety about the prospect of a nine-period day from next September and the implications of this for part-time and full-time colleagues. The lack of consultation and discussion by senior management has added to the frustration felt by many middle managers, and this is highlighted by the large number who seriously consider leaving teaching. In fact, the head of mathematics decided to take early retirement as his way of coping with the stress resulting from the reorganisation.

A head of a primary school was having considerable difficulties with:

> Unadaptable staff, whose resistance to all innovations in school whether concerned with induction, appraisal, INSET, initiatives from the Reform Act, length of school day or changes in staffroom furniture take the form of non-involvement, isolation from colleagues or cynicism.

The head of a secondary school was finding that the 'resisters' were presenting her with heavy management problems:

> A minority of staff have attempted to sabotage the system by outright antagonism to certain newly appointed staff and by becoming thoroughly unreasonable towards the pupils, both *en masse* and individually. The children are more reasonable, tolerant, loyal and forgiving than some staff. Some teachers are confused by consultation and long for a return to dictatorship and the 'close the doors and keep the nasty world out' syndrome. Stress comes from trying to maintain happy working relationships, not so much between the staff and me, but between warring factions of staff.

REDUCING RESISTANCE TO CHANGE

Plant recommends six key activities for managers to reduce resistance and to implement change effectively. These are:

- Provide help to face up to change.
- Communicate like never before.
- Work at gaining commitment.
- Ensure early involvement.
- Turn perception of 'threat' into opportunities.
- Avoid over-organising.

(Plant 1987: 32)

1 Provide help to face up to change

Plant emphasises the importance of 'avoiding the temptation to rush into offensive action and . . . spending some time listening and understanding' (Plant 1987: 31). He claims that 'the very process of listening actively to the resisting forces will have the effect of reducing them'.

> The head of Sixth Form was asked by two of the team of tutors if they could share some of the responsibilities of chairing team meetings. The head of Sixth Form was worried that these two experienced teachers might take over or direct the team towards objectives, discussions and actions with which he disagreed and he might lose control. After discussing his apprehensions with other course members, he agreed that the two tutors should have the delegated task of chairing their meetings. His follow-up reports to the course were very positive. He found he was more able to observe the team in action and to contribute his own ideas. He found his new role stimulating and he enjoyed the meetings.

The importance of patience in helping staff face up to change has also been noted by a number of managers taking part in my workshops. The principal of a Sixth Form college gives a good indication of the need for a patient, understanding and sensitive approach in the following report:

> My staff have all been redeployed to the college from local schools in which innovation, in terms of teaching methods, curriculum development and pastoral care, had been conspicuous by its absence in the main. The schools were all run with the termly or half-termly staff meeting as the only forum for discussion and advancement.
> As most of the staff are in their forties and fifties it has not been easy to alter this approach. Gradually such things as department meetings, working parties, and planning meetings are beginning to develop after 18 months and attaining a grudging acceptance as part of the job.

The deputy head of a secondary school noted:

> Curriculum change is desired by some staff but not by others. Time is needed to woo the conservative group, but the radicals are impatient. My job is to keep the waters calm, both sides talking and a goal in sight.

2 Communicate like never before

In Plant's second recommendation, the important task for managers is to give and receive as much information as possible, upwards, downwards and sideways. This reduces uncertainty and the risk of rumour and misinformation filling the vacuum caused by stoppages in the flow of information.

3 Work at gaining commitment

Managers should present the arguments for supporting the required changes as strongly as possible. They should emphasise their importance to the success, continuing development or even survival of the school. Plant encourages the development of a shared 'vision' in the organisation to promote commitment. But it is important not to let this process get out of hand, or it will take a huge slice of the human and time resources of the school. Readers may know this from their own experience, but the presentation shown in Figure 9.1 by the acting head of a secondary school may indicate some of the demands which can be made on governors and staff when they are developing a vision that is 'knowing where to go' (Kehoe 1993: 7).

It is important that in developing its vision of where it is going, by having a 'helicopter' perspective, a school does not lose sight of its immediate short-term concerns. Louise Kehoe in an article in *The Financial Times* states this risk quite clearly:

> Too much vision can also be a dangerous thing, as Apple Computer has discovered. While putting its energies into long-term innovative projects, such as Newton, Apple has failed to maintain the momentum of its core Macintosh personal computer business. Computer companies cannot afford to become so excited about the future that they lose focus on near-term issues and priorities.
>
> (Kehoe 1993: 7)

Her warning is surely relevant to schools as well as computer companies!

4 Ensure early involvement

Early involvement in the planning stage, Plant's fourth recommendation,

We need a restatement of the 'vision' for the future of the school and a long-term plan to realise that 'vision'. We are also agreed that there will be benefit in staff and governors working together on this process. I suggest that this can only be accomplished within an informed context and over a clear time span.

The issues

- We shall be forced to consider the essential 'character' of the school within the next few months.
- We shall have to develop a marketing strategy.
- We shall have to undertake a formal evaluation of our current aims and objectives.

The context

- We need a clear picture of the pattern of transfer from primary schools over the last five years.
- We need to see a range of possible financial scenarios based on the variations in the projected numbers entering the school and remaining in the Sixth Form over a period of five years.
- We shall need to know the cost of the revised shadow staffing structure and the actual structure from September 1993.
- We shall need to take account of current papers and policy from the LEA and the government, including the implications of likely decisions on single-sex transport.
- We shall need to consider the impact and future plans of our competitors.
- We shall have to be clear about our strategy for managing the implications of the demographic 'blip' in 1993/4.

© Routledge 1995

Figure 9.1 Developing a vision: presentation by acting head of a secondary school

is vital for effective change management. Encouraging staff to be actively involved in implementation and in providing essential feed-back information is also a vital management skill. A head of faculty strongly supported this recommendation:

As head of faculty at a time of radical change, one of my guiding principles has been to foster a team approach and a sense of working together within the faculty. We have been successful in implementing the National Curriculum and all the demands that follow in its wake because we have planned and executed our strategies together. Change imposed from outside creates uncertainty and anxiety.

In the past I had management experience of a different kind as the school IT Coordinator. The problems of trying to achieve changes right across the curriculum forced me to think hard about ways of achieving such changes. It is important to establish clear goals.

5 Turn perception of 'threat' into opportunities

Plant agrees that while managers should understand staff perception of some changes as threatening, they should also encourage the opportunity viewpoint. One of the issues included by the acting head in the proposal for developing a vision can be used as an example of the need for the manager to have a dual perspective – understanding of both the threats involved and the opportunities for staff contained in the statement 'We shall have to develop a marketing strategy'.

The threats perceived by staff include feelings of alienation from the values they see in the new business culture of the school, with its emphasis on competitive marketing activities in a free market for customers. Some of them are deeply sceptical of the educational value of what they are doing and the jargon involved, such as, for example, USP or 'Unique Selling Point'. They are hostile to a free-market philosophy for education in which 'primary and secondary schools are regarded as 2500 competing businesses obliged by the Government to scalp their competitors [and] the 'kill or be killed' ethic of the free market' (Wragg 1993: 52).

The head of a primary school expressed this perspective very clearly when he told the staff: 'We are going to have to sell ourselves to survive in a free market.'

So what opportunities are offered to teachers by these developments? Teachers on my courses are enthusiastic about these marketing initiatives, because they believe that there are many good things in mainstream schools that people never hear about. They argue that marketing skills can help schools improve their public relations and perhaps begin to change the derogatory images which many members of the public appear to have about schools and teachers. They suggest that marketing can be a cooperative enterprise, as schools in Essex and Devon have demonstrated. They believe that marketing and public relations are different names for similar concepts, and they responded positively to the invitation to complete the following exercise. Readers will also find it a useful analysis.

The fourth item listed – 'threat of closure' – was frequently included in the teachers' lists and they were interested to discuss a public relations programme prepared by the head of a primary school which had been nominated for closure. His initiatives included:

- Preparation of school dossier.
- Research and preparation of a document which gave the arguments for the survival of the school.

Below are some of the reasons why a school might need a public relations programme. Please tick any items which apply to your school.

Declining school rolls   [ ]
Retain pupils in or attract pupils to Sixth Form   [ ]
Poor school image   [ ]
Threat of closure   [ ]
Threat of cutbacks/need more resources   [ ]
Need to promote new policy   [ ]
Need for better home/school links   [ ]
Need for better links with some parents   [ ]
Need for better links with community   [ ]
Schools need better links with industry/business   [ ]
School has difficulty attracting the right kind of teachers   [ ]
Need to publicise a special occasion   [ ]
School does much good work but it goes unnoticed   [ ]
School wishes to wave the flag for its particular
    type (e.g. comprehensive, or single sex)   [ ]
Morale boost for staff   [ ]

© Routledge 1995

Training material 9.1 Reasons for a public relations programme

- Increase in report to governors (average of three governors' meetings per term). This, in a way, has been a good exercise in that it helps one reappraise one's values and principles in education.
- Press/TV/radio. Both local and national press and TV (plus schools radio) have taken an interest in our case and this has led to a considerable amount of time and energy being spent on press interviews, etc.
- 'Spreading the word'. The arguments of our case have been repeated over and over again to a variety of people in all walks of life. It is important to do this to gain the support we need.
- The parents. Although I have enjoyed considerable support from the parents, and this is a valuable resource, it has been paid for with a lot of diplomacy! This includes taking time to talk to individuals, making sure they are kept informed of developments and organising meetings in the evening.
- Governors. Again, these have been a source of support, but the extra liaison needed over the fight to save the school has caused extra worry and time consumption.

Marketing strategies also give teachers the opportunity to review the strengths of their school. They can have a beneficial impact on internal public relations to give a boost to staff morale. The review by a secondary school shown in Figure 9.2 reminded the staff of what they had achieved as well as bringing their achievements to the notice of parents, prospective parents, the media, services and associations in the city.

Before considering Plant's sixth and final recommendation, readers should take this opportunity to review the strengths of their school.

6 Avoid over-organising

Plant's final recommendation is that the change process is facilitated if organisations do not prepare the final plans in minute detail in the earliest stages of reorganisation. A broad framework is required but the detailed structures and procedures should be developed during the process and not at the beginning of it. This requires management flexibility of a high order.

Training

These six recommendations make a useful framework for managers. They are based on Plant's extensive experience as a management consultant. They can readily be applied to situations in primary and secondary schools. But there is one omission from his model which should be rectified by readers. This is the training of staff to assimilate the new initiatives required in their work.

Other management consultants write and hold workshops strongly advocating the urgent necessity of training and re-training. One of the most insistent of these is Tom Peters, and again and again in his book *Thriving on Chaos* he attempts to persuade his readers to train, train and keep on training (Peters 1988).

Staff support as a basis for change management

My own guidelines for effective change management have a different perspective from both Plant and Peters. They are meant to be used by the managed as well as by managers, which is a reflection of the whole-school approach to management on which this book is based:

- Teachers need to be informed and consulted about their opinions and feelings so they can be active participants in the changes that are affecting their work.
- They should participate with the head, senior management team and middle management in working out a careful strategy for change, which should be implemented in stages.

Our strengths

- a long-established reputation for high achievement and academic success;
- a single-sex education, which research has shown gives girls the best chance of achieving academic success;
- a commitment to achieving continuity and progression. There are well-organised induction programmes;
- a strong careers programme that ensures that pupils are highly successful in finding jobs, training opportunities or places in FE and HE;
- a reputation for outstanding success in Music, Art and Drama;
- a strong team of highly qualified, well-motivated, hard-working staff;
- a well-organised system of pastoral care, which promotes care and concern for the individual needs of pupils and ensures that they are known in depth;
- a well-organised programme of support for pupils who experience learning difficulties;
- a wide range of extra-curricular provision which gives pupils the opportunity to develop their full potential in non-academic areas. This includes residential experience, outdoor pursuits and visits abroad.

© Routledge 1995

Figure 9.2 Review of strengths of a secondary school

- They should be clear about their objectives and agree on realistic targets. When the first targets are achieved it is important that everyone's contribution is appreciated.
- They should make known their training needs and share their feelings.
- They should restrict any other changes that are not related to the Reform Act to the absolute minimum.
- They should share their disappointment if things do not happen as intended.
- Teachers should support their colleagues (including the head, senior management team or middle managers) if they need it and let their colleagues support them if they need it.

The most important conclusion from these guidelines is that it is essential for staff to support each other during the process of implementing the Reform Act, because they will only be fully successful in managing the initiatives if they share plans, problems and feelings.

Mutual staff support is also crucial in keeping under control one of the great barriers to effective change management: stress. How this control can be developed and maintained is one of the key strategies of the next chapter.

Chapter 10

Stress management

There is growing concern among teachers about the increasing mental, physical and emotional costs of stress at work. Their concern is reflected in the number of objectives related to stress which teachers want to achieve on my management courses, such as learning:

- how to avoid stress;
- coping strategies;
- how to help people smile and stay sane;
- how to improve the quality of life within school;
- how to reassure colleagues;
- survival skills;
- how to provide active support for colleagues.

This chapter uses these objectives as its targets and presents a framework to achieve them. Teachers have found it helpful in preparing, developing, practising and monitoring the beneficial effects of personal and whole school stress management programmes and policies. This framework has six parts:

- accepting the existence of stress in themselves and their colleagues caused by work pressures;
- learning to understand what stress is;
- beginning to tackle the problem by identifying the work pressures which are sources of stress;
- recognising the signs of stress which are the reaction to these negative pressures;
- identifying the coping strategies and resources which teachers use to reduce work pressures and the signs of stress;
- developing personal and whole-school stress management programmes and policies.

ACCEPTANCE OF STRESS

A primary teacher emphasised the importance of this first step in a stress management programme:

> I have learned not to be too proud to ask for help. I now know that acknowledging anxiety to yourself and expressing it to the right people is the first step in relieving it. Having had a complete breakdown I would plead with anyone to acknowledge stress long before it gets to that stage.

A secondary teacher wrote of the stigma which is still associated with stress:

> It seems to me that the most important aspect of coping with stress must be the recognition by an individual that stress is part of his/her problem. One's colleagues in the staffroom exhibit many symptoms which I would now associate with stress. I think that many of the sufferers would deny that they were prone to such weaknesses.

It is very difficult for colleagues who associate stress with failure, incompetence and weakness to make this first crucial move of recognition and acceptance. So for them the second stage in the programme can be very helpful.

LEARNING TO UNDERSTAND THE MEANING OF OCCUPATIONAL STRESS

This is important because staff have different definitions of stress and their perspective determines what they mean when they say they are or are not under stress. One view of stress which is common amongst teachers is to equate it with external pressures such as those coming from government initiatives or deadlines or poor working conditions. A second definition perceives stress as the reaction to these pressures – for example, emotional reactions like anger and physical reactions such as tension headaches. A third definition includes both pressures and reactions and also includes the coping resources and strategies which teachers use as they attempt to reduce their pressures and reactions. Stress from this perspective means a significant excess of pressures over resources and strategies which leads to the development of behavioural, emotional, mental and physical stress reactions. This is the definition used in my workshops and in this chapter.

BEGINNING TO TACKLE THE PROBLEM

The first step in reducing stress is to identify which work pressures are sources of stress. Before each of my workshops staff are invited to complete a questionnaire about their work. The first three questions are:

- What does your work involve?
- Which parts of your work do you find acceptable and enjoyable?
- What pressures of your work cause the greatest problems for you and your colleagues?

Readers should now answer these questions as if they were completing a questionnaire before a stress management workshop. They should then compare their answers to the second question – which parts of your work do you find acceptable and enjoyable? – with the following answers to the same question given by staff in a secondary school preparing for an INSET day:

- 'I enjoy the variety of work.'
- 'Pressure which has a clean finishing point.'
- 'Pressure with a purpose.'
- 'Most of the administration if I have enough warning of deadlines so that I can comfortably achieve it before the appointed time.'
- 'Teaching – I relish this part of my job more and more.'
- 'I enjoy most of it. I like working with both staff and pupils.'

A group of eight deputy heads of primary schools also preparing for an INSET workshop gave the following replies to the same question:

- 'Organising events/in-service days.'
- 'Being in my classroom for a whole day uninterrupted.'
- 'Any legitimate tasks that can be completed successfully.'
- 'Problem solving within my job: children, curriculum or parents.'
- 'Constant changes in the class dynamics; every day is different.'
- 'Planning topic work.'
- 'My curriculum responsibilities.'
- 'Working with the senior management team.'
- 'LMS, when given the appropriate time and access to the necessary information.'
- 'Class teaching and doing things with the children, especially creative activities.'
- 'Workload: I like to be busy.'
- 'New challenges.'
- 'Creative work.'
- 'Being involved at the centre, making decisions, having a say on many issues, feeling valued, working with children.'

Positive work pressures are not sources of stress for teachers. They are very significant coping strategies and resources providing the uplifts to sustain staff as they encounter the negative work pressures which are sources of stress. These replies from primary and secondary teachers indicate that when it creates positive pressures work itself can be a coping resource, as well as a source of stress for teachers. But the negative work pressures as well as the positive must be investigated, and the third in the questionnaire is: 'What pressures of your work cause the greatest problems for you and your colleagues?'. The replies of the secondary school staff to this question included:

- 'Sheer volume of work. It appears to be never ending. Having so much to do means that it does not all get done properly.'
- 'Always having to go home in the evening to work is most depressing. One could be totally consumed by work.'
- 'Lack of communication from other staff.'
- 'Getting behind with organisation and marking in my department because of pressures elsewhere.'
- 'Keeping up with the heavy demands of the National Curriculum.'
- 'Horrendous load of paperwork.'
- 'Some meetings become endlessly repetitive or too long and I am not in a position to do anything about it.'
- 'My inability to cope with unreasonable people.'
- 'Other staff failing to meet deadlines which affects my ability to meet a subsequent deadline.'
- 'I have never found the pressures as great as they are this year.'

The replies of the primary school deputy heads identified the following pressures as sources of stress:

- 'So many tasks that cannot be properly dealt with and completed lead to feelings of incompetence.'
- 'The job requires so much time now that it intrudes into all aspects of the rest of my life.'
- 'Becoming the scapegoat for things which have gone wrong at work.'
- 'Staff illness, which causes uncertainty and worry for me, often during the weekend.'
- 'Role conflict because of being class teacher and deputy head, leading to dissatisfaction with the results of either role.'
- 'It is the smaller issues that build up, leading to a time of being stressed.'

Will readers now please identify work pressures which are sources of stress for them. They can then compare them with the replies of the primary and secondary teachers.

More information about negative work pressures has been presented in small-scale action research projects in their own secondary schools by teachers on my Bristol University courses. They asked their colleagues to put in rank order of importance as sources of stress ten pressures which had been identified in a research project involving 1,790 teachers in the

United Kingdom by researchers at the University of Manchester Institute of Science and Technology (Travers and Cooper 1990). These researchers identified in rank order the ten top sources of occupational stress in teaching as:

- lack of support from Government;
- constant changes;
- lack of information about these changes;
- lack of respect for teachers;
- National Curriculum;
- salaries out of proportion with workload;
- pupil assessment;
- pupils' behavioural problems;
- lack of non-contact time;
- lack of relation between teaching skill and promotion.

The teachers' projects found different rank orders of these items and additional sources of stress. The results from three schools in rank order were:

- constant changes;
- National Curriculum;
- lack of information about changes;
- lack of non-contact time;
- lack of Government support;
- pupil assessment;
- lack of relationship between teaching skill and promotion;
- lack of respect for teachers;
- salaries out of proportion to workload;
- pupils' behavioural problems.

Members of staff in these schools also cited lack of senior management competence and understanding; administration; financial constraints; increasing variety of tasks; appraisal; and lack of support from colleagues.

The course member in one of these three schools made some perceptive observations about changes in the causes of stress for his colleagues:

> Several readers I talked to looked at the list and said 'but I always knew it would be like that'. In other words, they were prepared for the stress associated with these factors and equipped themselves with the necessary skills to be able to cope with them. What is undoubtedly new is the rapid increase in some of the factors associated with the pace of change in education that has been experienced over the past few years. The rate of policy change, the introduction of new initiatives, the threat of redeployment are new and severe stressors. Many teachers feel that the goalposts are constantly being moved and many lack the resources to be able to cope with this.

The course member in another school came to the conclusion that:

> The crux of the problem seems to be that teachers have less control over the curriculum and their own futures while at the same time they are being held increasingly accountable to their managers and the public. Add to this the increasing dichotomy between the philosophy of teachers and the government, poor rewards in terms of salary and promotion prospects and low status in the public eye, and we paint a very bleak picture of the stress levels of teachers.

Another course member was particularly interested in the stress of middle managers, as she explained in her project report:

> In order to get a clearer view of the types of stress experienced by middle managers, I conducted a survey in my own school. The response to a questionnaire that I issued was very good. I received three replies from the five year heads and seven replies from the eight faculty heads. I asked each person to list some pressures that existed for them in school which caused them stress and to place them, if they could, in rank order. Not everyone was able to produce a rank order as some pointed out that the pressures often varied from day to day. Perhaps not surprisingly the three year heads had lack of parental support high on their lists, but shared the feeling along with the faculty heads that the senior management team is a major source of stress in the school! One head of year felt that she was excluded from any real decisions that are made and that there was a definite us and them situation. This failure to achieve a feeling of corporate identity of wide ownership of the school even among middle managers leads to high stress levels. There was a difference in the pressures felt by the most recently appointed faculty heads compared with those who had been there some time. Two of the three more recently appointed commented on the problems of dealing with disillusioned staff in their faculties. One of the recently appointed told me: 'I seem to spend a lot of my time verbally massaging the members of my faculty'.
>
> But the long-standing faculty heads have different pressures, for example, the emergence of new subjects and the amalgamation of others. This is a source of major pressure for a colleague who was originally head of the Craft Faculty. He is now head of Design Technology and is finding the swing away from technical skills in favour of design a big problem.

These reports from different schools show the value of small school-based action research projects conducted by members of staff for the identification of work pressures which are sources of occupational stress. Programmes and policies to reduce these identified pressures can then be prepared, developed and implemented.

The importance of bringing these into operation as soon as possible will be very clear as the next stage in my six-part stress management programme is reached.

RECOGNISING THE SIGNS OF STRESS

To help staff to achieve this objective they are invited to respond to the question: How do you react if your attempts to reduce work pressure are ineffective?. Staff in a secondary school preparing for an in-service stress management workshop, whose work pressures were identified earlier in this chapter, gave the following responses to this question:

- 'I find sustained thought or concentration difficult.'
- 'I suppose I get worries and moan more to other people.'
- 'I feel angry and frustrated.'
- 'Psoriasis.'
- 'Stomach knots up.'
- 'Sometimes irritable bowel syndrome.'
- 'Moodiness and irritability.'

The signs of stress reported by the deputy heads of primary schools were:

- 'I get short tempered, intolerant, tense and aggressive.'
- 'I find it difficult to listen to others' problems or appreciate their needs.'
- 'I become less effective in my job.'
- 'I am unable to break out of the downward spiral; even if I know what I should do I cannot bring myself to do it.'
- 'I become withdrawn from what is going on around me.'
- 'I avoid people.'

The course members who investigated the pressures on staff in their schools also asked their colleagues to indicate on a checklist which signs of stress they had experienced. The staff responses in three schools are shown in Table 10.1.

The teachers in School A added four more signs of stress to their checklists, namely long-term illness, increased probability of error, loss of memory and irritable bowel syndrome. The teachers in School C added the following to their lists: frustration, headaches and hypersensitivity to criticism.

Each of the course members in these three schools added to the value of their numerical data by making useful and interesting observations. The teacher–researcher in School A commented:

Many of my colleagues seem to find it comforting that they were not the only ones suffering from a particular stress-related ailment. Many

Table 10.1 Percentage of staff identifying stress reactions

Signs of stress	School A %	School B %	School C %
Large increase in consumption of alcohol	15	12	12
Marital/family conflict	35	24	12
Marked reduction of contact with people outside school	31	64	18
Displaced aggression on to children, partners, colleagues and others outside school	38	48	18
Apathy	31	48	18
Wanting to leave teaching	46	52	5
Irritability	50	72	47
Moodiness	23	36	0
Strong feelings of being unable to cope	12	32	23
Inability to take decisions	23	28	12
Feverish activity with little purpose	15	36	12
Inability to concentrate	27	36	5
Depression	19	40	0
Anger	35	28	18
Anxiety	27	32	18
Loss of sleep	35	52	35
Loss of weight	0	12	0
Feelings of guilt	12	32	18
Overeating	23	32	29
Large increase in smoking	0	4	18
Back pain	19	36	12
Withdrawal from staff contact	19	36	12
Absenteeism	4	8	0
Feelings of exhaustion	69	52	23
Feelings of isolation in school	19	48	12

of the respondents were willing to relate that their reactions to stress were increasing. Many told me that they had actually felt under great stress over the last few years, especially since the advent of the National Curriculum and its associated demands. Many felt that their reactions to stress were becoming more extreme.

The report from the course member in School B noted:

I see in the staffroom and in meetings irritability, poor humour, moodiness, reluctance to make decisions, hectic but seemingly purposeless activity, inability to concentrate. These I believe are all signs of stress. Colleagues I know well admit to insomnia, taking time off, domestic conflict, heavy drinking and/or smoking and frequent use of tranquilisers. I would now suggest that many of these are symptomatic of occupational stress.

The crucial interaction between stress reactions and coping resources and strategies was commented on by the teacher–researcher in School C. She was attempting to understand the lower levels of reported stress in her school compared with other surveys:

> My perception of the school is of one with a high level of mutual support between all grades of staff and this greatly reduces the potential stress from poorly motivated, less able and disruptive pupils. The school culture also gives a relatively high degree of control to staff, which gives them a feeling of control of the situation and hence reduces stress. Also the school does not tend to jump on bandwagons but weighs up the benefits to pupils before embarking upon change. It would seem from the results of the survey on the stress reaction of staff that middle managers are suffering less stress than teaching or non-teaching staff. This could suggest that middle managers have developed successful coping strategies for themselves but they are not always helping their staff to do the same. Alternatively it could mean that middle managers are less stressed because they have a relatively high degree of control in a small institution and are not involved in the stronger hierarchical system of a bigger school.

These reports of stress symptoms from primary and secondary teachers have indicated a significant discrepancy between the pressures experienced by staff and their coping resources and strategies. To reduce stress it is necessary to reduce these pressures and strengthen resources. The stress management programme seeks to help staff find out what coping resources they have, and, working from this resource audit, seeks to rectify any gaps that have been discovered by whole-school and personal stress management programmes and policies. First we will consider Part 5 of the programme.

IDENTIFYING AND SHARING THE COPING STRATEGIES AND RESOURCES TO REDUCE STRESS

The secondary teachers preparing for their INSET day gave a number of detailed and wide-ranging reports of the actions they took at school and at home. Five reports are included here:

- 'I set aside "family time" with my boys from 5–8pm before starting working etc. I try to encourage my husband to join in functions to

which I am required to go. He is in the school choir and comes to some social occasions. I work late most nights, until midnight or later. I make lists and cross things off to make myself feel good. I do crossword puzzles before I go to sleep to "switch off" and then sleep like a log!'
- 'Often I take the initiative and try to change the system. It's a slow process, but it gives me a feeling of being in control! Sometimes I take a walk at lunchtime with a friend, and have a good moan!'
- 'I play sport or swim or walk up hills and try to avoid my husband winding me up. We go abroad on holiday if we can manage it, as that is the only time I am not in contact with school.'
- 'I delegate where possible but all the members of my department are as busy as I am! I have been to the head and told him that I could not cope with the job, which was extremely effective. Communication and telling the truth are great reducers of tension.'
- 'I take boxes of Ginseng.'

Primary school deputy heads identified the coping strategies they used in school as:

- 'Completing a limited number of tasks.'
- 'Doing anything that can be done straight away, straight away!'
- 'Talking to colleagues who share my views of what is important in the job.'
- 'Talking about the pressures with head and senior management team.'
- 'Getting on with the job in hand.'
- 'Talking to head – we have a very good relationship.'

These primary deputy heads identified their outside school strategies as:

Relaxing baths, running, aromatherapy oils, reading Agatha Christie, keeping fit, sport, doing something completely different and unrelated to work, physical activity, reading, making time for myself, having a calming down time when I first get home, always taking Sunday off and usually going for a walk or a pub lunch, switching off at home, cutting grass in the garden, making time for my family such as bathing my daughter, cutting off from school with my young family in the evening, talking to husband: all activities put problems into perspective, off-load the problems of the day on to the family.

The teachers in schools A, B and C were invited by the teacher–researcher in their schools to identify their coping strategies on a checklist. Their answers are presented in Table 10.2 in the rank order that staff identified them.

These reports of primary and secondary teachers' attempts to reduce the harmful effects of stress have identified a wide range of skills, knowledge, techniques, relationships, thoughts and activities which can be

Table 10.2 Rank order of coping strategies

Coping strategies	School A	School B	School C
Deciding priorities	1	1	2
Working evenings and weekends	2	9	1
Planning well ahead	3	10	3
Talking to colleagues	4	3	6
Hobby to get away from school mentally	5	5	12
Preparing and marking less well than I would like	6	10	15
Becoming more philosophical: do what you can but do not worry too much	7	6	5
Catching up with family life in holidays	8	3	14
Dropping low-priority school tasks	9	2	7
Exercising	10	10	13
Developing different styles of teaching	11	8	10
Working harder	12	6	4
Working 9-5 then forgetting about the job	13	15	16
Relaxed breathing	14	16	17
Saying * * * the school work and going out	15	13	8
More sporting activities	18	14	9
Muscle relaxation	17	18	11
Making compromises	16	17	18

classified as personal, interpersonal, organisational and community resources. Personal resources include work strategies, positive attitudes,
positive work pressures and out-of-work activities. Many of the resources
included in the reports are personal, including:

- 'Prioritising.'
- 'Often I take the initiative and try to change the system.'
- 'Developing different styles of teaching to enable me to cope with a
  continuous stretch of it.'
- 'Doing something completely different and unrelated to work.'

Interpersonal resources include:

- 'Cutting off from school with my young family in the evening.'
- 'Sometimes taking a walk at lunchtime with a friend and having a
  good moan!'

Organisational resources include:

- 'Talking to colleagues who share my views of what is important in the job.'
- 'Talking about the pressures with the head and senior management team.'

Community resources mentioned in the reports are:

- 'Always taking Sunday off and usually going for a walk or a pub lunch.'
- 'Having more sporting activities.'
- 'Walking up hills!'

Organisational resources and strategies appear to be considerably rarer for these primary and secondary teachers than personal or interpersonal ones. Support from the head and the senior management team is reported by teachers but support from colleagues in the staffroom is more frequently available. The value of staff support was very clearly argued by the teacher–researcher in school C when she wrote:

> My perception of the school is of one with a high level of mutual support between all grades of staff and this greatly reduces the potential stress from poorly motivated, less able and disruptive pupils.

The recognition of a weakness in organisational resources is a strong argument for the final part of the six-part framework.

DEVELOPING PERSONAL AND WHOLE SCHOOL STRESS MANAGEMENT PROGRAMMES AND POLICIES

This focus should include personal/interpersonal strategies such as relaxation, exercise, cognitive restructuring, visualisation, assertiveness training and time management. All these approaches can help staff to reduce the pain, worry and sickness of stress. These skills can be incorporated in the whole-school programme and information about them can be found in Dunham (1992).

But the programme should also use a stress audit of pressures, stress reactions and coping strategies, as we have discussed in this chapter. Analysis should lead not to paralysis but to action. The review should be the framework and the motivator for training. Following the identification of the major work pressures on teaching and non-teaching staff and the recognition of the signs of stress there should be the opportunity for staff to articulate their coping strategies and for the school to identify its strengths and training needs for the core of staff.

The coping strategies checklist from Schools A, B and C should be used for this purpose. Each school should review its rank order and consider whether changes in the regular use of strategies would be beneficial – for example, in School A strategy 2, working evenings and weekends, might be given less priority and strategy 9, dropping low-priority school tasks, could be used more frequently.

Organisational resources should also be strengthened by developing whole-school policies and programmes based on the recommendations made by teachers for reducing stress in their schools. Information about them can be found in their answers to the final question in the stress management questionnaire: What are your recommendations for reducing stress in school for you and your colleagues?

Many of the secondary teachers' answers suggested they believed their stress would be reduced if the management skills of the senior management team were improved. This is clearly expressed in the following recommendations:

- 'More awareness from the executive of what is happening on the ground would save a tremendous amount of frustration and therefore stress.'
- 'The management team should plan ahead and attempt to avoid late decisions which mess up our teaching programme.'
- 'Meetings should be more effective and there should be a fortnightly staff newsletter to replace the present method of communication at staff meetings.'
- 'Have a selection process which ensures a better fit between person and job.'
- 'More money should be invested in training so as to develop more confidence in the job.'
- 'Team-work, which provides group support, should be encouraged.'
- 'Teachers' roles should be reviewed to minimise confusion, conflict and overload.'

The teacher–researchers in Schools A, B,and C all made important observations and recommendations which should be discussed by readers and their colleagues actively and thoroughly. Their recommendations were very much concerned with the roles of middle managers. The teacher–researcher in School A made a strong case for recognising the key roles which middle managers should and could play in whole-school approaches:

The middle manager is ideally placed to observe both the individual and the organisational elements, and to incorporate them into a coping resource to be used for the benefit of individuals, the team and the institution.

The implications of a failure of middle managers to recognise and deal with stress in themselves and their teams are enormous. The build-up of stressors over recent years means that without the necessary coping strategies, more teachers will suffer stress-related conditions. Effective middle managers hold the key to promoting the adoption of coping resources. They know their teams, they are aware of the limits that their teams can operate within, and they are able to deal with their teams' stress because they have the ability to deal with their own. My conclusions to this investigation take the form of recommendations. I would suggest the following firm steps are taken to allow middle managers in particular to develop the coping resources necessary to tip the balance in favour of well-being in themselves and their teams.

Those in middle management roles should be given training in personal, interpersonal and organisational skills for reducing individual and group stress. Those seeking promotion to middle management positions should follow similar training.

- Organisations should actively encourage the setting up of support groups.
- All staff should receive training on stress management techniques and on identifying stress causes and reactions.
- The training advocated should be part of a staff development INSET programme and should follow a stress audit of teams and the whole school.

The report from the teacher–researcher in School B presents guidelines for middle management to be effective in managing their own stress and supporting their colleagues:

It is important for middle managers fully to understand the complexity of their role, which has changed and developed fairly rapidly over the last few years. It is a highly skilled one, which usually involves a large managerial role combined with a heavy teaching load. In the case of the pastoral care heads, their role involves a heavy teaching load combined with administration, discipline and liaising with outside agencies. Anyone doing this demanding job needs to be flexible and well organised. The middle manager is often a key person when changes are being introduced. This may put them in a position where they are on the receiving end of other people's stress. Their role is also difficult because they act as an intermediary between the team and the senior management of the school. Good middle managers need to be able to cope with their own pressures, while at the same time helping to reduce the stress on the team. Stress is not just a personal matter. It can also have a domino effect, for example, one team member undergoing severe stress can put the cohesion of the whole team at risk if this is not managed sensitively. The middle manager has to be able to deal with other people's stress and have a strategy to cope with it. This does not mean absorbing that stress but, through listening, finding ways to support one's colleagues.

It is essential to keep a multi-track mind so that the job does not become your whole life. The workaholic middle manager on the road to burnout is all too common these days. It is necessary to develop interests outside school and to take exercise. Having a multi-track mind also means building in time to reflect and stand back from your role from time to time. It is a key strategy to adopt a balanced approach to one's job; both personal and family life are important. Middle managers should accept their strengths and limitations. Middle managers should be available to their team, but they should also create time to withdraw to work on specific tasks, and to reflect. It is vital to get this balance right. It is a good coping strategy to be able to share responsibility and to delegate tasks. It is not a good coping strategy to try to do everything yourself. Trusting people to take some of the responsibility is a key part of the middle manager's role. Having an overview of a team does not mean making all key decisions yourself, it means listening and being aware of the work that the team is doing and helping them to work out an effective strategy to move forward. It is important to praise team colleagues and to build on the success of the team.

Middle managers have a responsibility to provide different types of support to members of their team. This might range from a weekly meeting with a probationary teacher to delegating parts of their management role to another member of the team who is interested in taking on more responsibility. Middle managers have to be sensitive to the pressures on particular people and within certain constraints give them special consideration, such as an appropriate time-table or spread of classes. It is also vital that they receive appropriate training about running meetings, appraisal, time management and good communications. They should constantly be updating their skills.

The report from School C includes a specific proposal which is strongly recommended:

Each school should have a stress management committee to look at ways of enhancing the quality of life in the institution for both staff and pupils. Such a committee should be fairly high-powered, but it should not be dominated by senior management. There should be representative members from every level of responsibility and faculty. The committee should also include non-teaching staff.

This recommendation for support staff involvement is important because in a whole school model of staff care the support staff are fully integrated in the stress management programme and in the development of support groups. In a whole school model they share with the teaching staff:

- access to the staffroom and its facilities;
- representation on the governing body;
- consultation about matters in which they have an interest – for example, a whole-school no-smoking policy;
- regular meetings.

(Warrington 1993)

These recommendations complete the range of personal, interpersonal, organisational and community resources which have been discussed in this chapter. They provide a sound basis for readers wanting to learn to deal with work pressures and stress reactions more effectively. There has been a focus on what middle management can do to contribute to whole-school models of staff care. But this perspective should not bring extra burdens on middle management. Staff care should be the concern of all support and teaching staff and should not be thought of as an exclusive responsibility of senior and middle management. My research suggests that they, too, need support from their colleagues (Dunham 1992). So it is essential that the skills of coping be shared by staff in what the teacher–researcher in School B has called a 'sharing–learning culture'.

Middle managers have a great and perhaps unique opportunity, because they are recognised by staff as 'one of us', to strengthen this culture by sharing in the development of whole-school policies and pro-grammes for stress reduction and prevention. They can also make this culture stronger and more accessible to all teaching and support staff by the use of the management skills reviewed in this book. There is often an inverse relationship between management skills and staff stress: good management brings less stress but poor management results in more stress. My comments and conclusions about these skills are presented in the next chapter.

Chapter 11

Conclusion

The need for training and yet more training for middle managers is my major conclusion. This need was expressed very clearly in the previous chapter by the teacher–researcher from school B, who is a middle manager:

> It is important for middle managers fully to understand the complexity of their role, one which has changed and developed rapidly over the past few years. It is a highly skilled role which usually involves a large managerial component combined with a heavy teaching load.

One highly significant cause of this training gap has been the perception of many headteachers that middle managers do not need specific management training; consequently they are allowed an inadequate amount of non-contact time to carry out their managerial tasks. In Chapter 1 there was a brief discussion of a 1993 School Teachers' Review Body Report which was critical of senior management teams which were weak in several key aspects of management (TES 1993: 6). One such weakness was the failure to make full use of those in middle management positions. The Review Body also criticised the low level of non-contact time for those with coordinators' responsibilities.

THE IMPORTANCE OF ON-SITE MANAGEMENT DEVELOPMENT

In my courses and in this book a significant focus of management training to fill this gap has been on enabling members and readers to find learning opportunities in their own past and present work experience. It is very important that these opportunities are continually looked for in, and provided by, their day-to-day experiences in school as the major part of their continuing professional development. Their main source of learning the essential management skills is, therefore, within the everyday life of the school. The chapters of this book are simply the facilitating agents.

A similar view is presented in a booklet published by Shropshire Education Department:

The development of management expertise is an important contribution to professional growth and is best achieved when the whole
staff is involved in school development and management. That notion
requires a shift of perception about who are the managers from head
and deputy and, perhaps, postholders to everyone including the newest
recruit. Each has a responsibility and each has therefore an entitlement
to management training.

(Shropshire Education Department 1993: 3)

Berkshire Education Department's publication *Developing Managers*
(Berkshire LEA 1991) provided the inspiration for this Shropshire
booklet. The principles, also well argued in the National Development
Centre's handbook *Management Development and Educational Reform*
(McMahon and Bolam 1990), are that:

- All teachers are managers.
- Management expertise is an entitlement.
- Senior managers have a duty to foster the development of others.
- Management strategies and development skills are learned on the
  job, supported by colleagues, as much as from traditional INSET
  activities.
- Personal development goes hand-in-hand with school development.

(Shropshire Education Department 1993: 3)

Two words might well be added to the third item on the list. This
principle would then read: 'Senior managers have a duty to foster the
development of others and themselves!'.

The whole-school, on-site model of professional development for
teaching and support staff has a wide range of training methods and
learning resources available. These may include:

- distance learning materials from the Open University, the National
  Development Centre for School Management Training (NDC), and the
  Henley Distance Learning Centre;
- using role models;
- coaching;
- delegating;
- observation of management styles as suggested in Chapter 2;
- having a mentor;
- shadowing;
- rotating the chair of meetings;
- sharing presentations to parents, governors and others;
- buying in the services of consultants for workshops, courses, conferences, stress management counselling;
- INSET within department or pastoral teams as well as for the whole
  school;

- using materials from off-site courses, with those members of staff who have attended acting as facilitators;
- rotating the membership of the senior management team by the inclusion of members of middle management for a period;
- developing quality circles, with open membership of teaching and support staff to investigate specific issues and make recommendations;
- the use of staff library facilities;
- 'rehearsals' for interviews for those applying for posts elsewhere;
- self-directed facilities using audio- and video-tapes for interactive learning.

Problem solving is one of the most effective methods of learning. The following report from the head of a science faculty shows how situations creating considerable difficulties for teaching and support staff can become good opportunities for professional and organisational growth.

Within the science faculty a central problem arose which hinged on resource availability. The Attainment Target Sc1 of the National Curriculum requires increased practical work for students, especially those beginning Key Stage 3 in Year 7. This called for a complete review of our teaching and learning styles with the result that we recognised the need for more open access of resources.

The availability of resources directly affected the efficiency of the technicians' working time. The preparation room became a nightmare with everything being needed at once. The technicians were fully stretched by this and lost valuable time for stock control, maintenance and repair. Their morale rapidly deteriorated under stress and their brusque behaviour contributed to teacher stress. The knock-on effect on students became evident: curriculum and pastoral problems emerged. Attempting to support all parties while keeping the students' needs to the fore at all times felt like a betrayal of each party.

The solution came about from the recognition that resources could be continually available as modularised packages on trolleys. Funding was made available to provide the trolleys but these were found to take up valuable space in an otherwise already crowded preparation room. An extension was required. Consultation with the senior management team enabled this to be identified as a faculty target within the development plan and I requested that it be a focus of attention in the forthcoming review by Advisers. At this the Senior Adviser agreed that our plan to extend the preparation room into the adjacent Technology Faculty's woodstore was a sensible proposition. However, since the proposal affected another faculty it required continuous consultation with the senior management team and the governors. They regularly visited the preparation room, talked to teaching and technical staff and helped to put the structural plan on paper.

Technician morale was raised as a result of the governors and senior management team talking directly with them and listening to their problems. Approval of the enlargement of the preparation room was a boost to all: teaching staff could see the light at the end of the tunnel and their morale was raised. With this additional space, teaching staff began to plan their practical work in the preparation room and more frequent constructive dialogue with the technicians took place. Each party began to feel more supported by the other, teamwork improved and student learning took on a more favourable pace.

As a final note, the technology faculty was delighted that it obtained a new, slightly larger, woodstore closer to its workshop. What had been one faculty's problem had worked to the advantage of two faculties.

The advantages of whole school, on-site management development and training can be appreciable and well worth the reader's attention when considering professional development programmes. They can be much less costly for staff in terms of their time and energy and for the school in terms of their expense. They can be tailor-made to relate directly to identified staff needs. For example, one secondary headteacher, in reviewing the introduction of appraisal, concluded a report to staff thus: 'We have assembled a list of INSET needs and are beginning to implement them. A need has emerged for training aspiring middle management.'

There is another advantage in these on-site learning approaches: the increase of the general level of staff awareness of good management practice in such skills as teamwork, time management, delegation or the management of meetings. With training, staff come to know what good management is and, in situations where they are suffering from poor management, they are able to articulate what they believe the required improvements might be. Management for all should raise the quality of pupil learning and the overall conduct of the school. This means that all members of staff must accept responsibility for achieving high-quality management and not leave that responsibility to the senior management team or middle managers. Teamwork is a good example of this requirement: all team members need to know how to achieve satisfying and successful teamwork.

THE BENEFITS OF OFF-SITE MANAGEMENT DEVELOPMENT

These advantages suggest that this model of staff development should be recommended and widely adopted. This does not mean that the alternative off-site model of attending courses, conferences and workshops should be written off in the mistaken belief that they have nothing to offer. Teachers who have been members of my university courses report advantages in this method of professional development:

- meeting people from a variety of schools and a variety of educational backgrounds;
- having a taste of the academic life again, stretching one's mind, learning new concepts and writing academic essays again.

Teachers sometimes need to be in a learning group away from their schools. For the teacher whose comment appears below, the course became a strong support group and her report shows the benefits she received:

> For me the course could not have come at a more appropriate time. Just before the course began I had in a sense failed to get a job which I really wanted in a school in which I really liked teaching. When the course started I was finding it very difficult to accept the changes which were beginning to take place in that school. I felt undervalued and very much a failure. My anger was being further influenced by my being often told what an excellent classroom teacher I was. Because of my feelings of failure, this was something I found difficult to come to terms with. As a result, at school I became quite cynical and probably was not always the best person to be around.
>
> Having the support of other colleagues on the course, and being able to share in some of their disappointments, helped me to come to terms with things. Much of the course also helped me to clarify a great deal of my previous understanding and, with time, this certainly contributed to the rebuilding of my self-confidence and eventually my self-esteem.

The following objectives of course members identified at the beginning of their course also give an indication of the value of off-site learning opportunities as they saw them:

- time to reflect;
- the opportunity to meet people from other schools in order to share their experience;
- the opportunity to consider in depth the issues raised in order to perform better;
- becoming more aware of a wider range of management styles.

These objectives show the importance teachers attach to extending their knowledge and skills by using the experience of peer teachers in other schools. They need the time and the opportunity to reflect upon what they hear, to ask questions and to become able to use what they are discovering.

The last objective on the list is a very relevant example. Teachers' experience of management styles in school is restricted to the role models they have encountered in their previous and present schools, even those in which they were themselves pupils. To extend their range of possible management styles by learning from colleagues is a major advantage of off-site courses.

RECOMMENDATIONS FOR EFFECTIVE TRAINING

It is not my intention to recommend one method rather than another. A very experienced user of both concluded: 'Either can be very good, or equally very bad.' In order for either type of learning experience to provide excellent opportunities for professional growth it is essential that they satisfy the following criteria for successful learning:

- The objectives of the chosen training method should relate directly to the identified training needs of the learners.
- There should be a 'good fit' between teaching style and learning style.
- Teaching styles within a course should be as varied as possible to meet the wide range of training and personal needs.
- The personal needs may include the raising of confidence, better inter-personal skills, improved self-esteem or reduced feelings of isolation.
- There should be periodic reviews of the items in this criteria checklist. The evaluation should not be left to the end of the course or training experience.
- Successful learning requires that as many learning experiences as possible be provided to enable members to share their skills, knowledge and attitudes. In an off-site course it is essential for bridges to be built with the members' schools. One way is to invite course members to choose a mentor within their school who will regularly review and discuss with them the course work programme, materials and discussion outcomes. Often on my courses this mentor is a member of the senior management team.
- Programmes for either method should be adaptable as fresh training needs emerge and the course progresses.

FILLING THE TRAINING GAPS OF TQM AND QA

These on-site and off-site recommendations are relevant to any attempt to fill a training gap in professional development. One of the biggest of these gaps, which managers are under much pressure to close, lies in the field of total quality management (TQM). This has been defined as 'creating the conditions that make continuous improvements possible' (Arkin 1993: 4). Arkin believes that TQM is all about 'finding ways of satisfying customers' (Arkin 1993: 4).

Customers are both internal to the organisation and external, and Arkin reports that one secondary school's response to the need to 'satisfy customers' was to set up a customer satisfaction group. Part of this group's role was to make a survey of Sixth Form opinions about their courses and discuss this survey with the students and their parents. The headteacher, the senior management team and some school governors have attended courses run by IBM (UK) on TQM.

Merrick has reported that in a primary school the headteacher and four colleagues went on 'four days of awareness training . . . to discover what quality assurance was about' (Merrick 1993: 6). The headteacher concerned had shared with her husband, a design manager in heating and ventilation, her concerns about discipline within the school. He suggested 'that the school should look into BS 5750 as a means of improving accountability and tightening up its management structure' (Merrick 1993: 5). The school applied to the British Standards Institution for details of registration for this extremely rigorous form of quality assurance (QA). This was the first school in the country to seek this registration, which had previously been confined to industry and commerce. After 14 months of drafting and continuing dialogue with the BSI, the school finally produced its application, in the form of a 25-page booklet on the school's management system and a second booklet of 80 pages which included 35 procedures, adapted from industry, for performing functions within the school. Thus the procedure 'corrective action' led to the senior management team introducing a monthly meeting to discuss internal and external complaints and to look at any recurring problems. Merrick reports: 'Assessors from BSI visited the school for two full days: to check that the school was putting the procedures manual into practice . . . . The assessors found forty minor areas of non-compliance' [which the school put right within two weeks] (Merrick 1993: 6). Merrick found that the school was convinced that the 'time, money (for registration, certification and consultancy fees) and the effort were all worthwhile' (ibid.). The staff told him that working to BS 5750 produced 'a more effectively managed school where roles and responsibilities are clearly defined and teachers can feel more confident about delivering the curriculum' (ibid.).

These positive responses to TQM and QA approaches in schools are supported by much more extensive planning and the implementation of quality systems and processes by a number of LEAs. Progress reports from two LEAs, Birmingham and Bradford, make good reading (Simkins et al. 1992). These developments are a clear indication of the training gap and learning vacuum which existed before these quality initiatives became available. The models were of necessity industrial because none had previously been created for education. One teacher in the primary school that was accredited by BSI told Merrick: 'Until we started to monitor the delivery of the curriculum against the criteria we had set there was no way of picking up any gaps. Now we can ensure that all areas of the curriculum are being covered' (Merrick 1993: 6).

It is very important that what is happening in the USA with TQM in industry does not happen in this country in education. Albrecht predicts that TQM will be out of vogue and unwanted in three years' time. He bases this prediction on his findings that:

> One organization after another has flirted with TQM and found it cumbersome, time-consuming and lacking in focus . . . as one corporate TQM program after another fizzles, founders, runs aground or grinds to a halt, disappointing its hopeful creators and implementers.
>
> (Albrecht 1992: 1)

To preserve our concern for quality in management development we should follow these guidelines:

- identify the problems or barriers to implementation;
- recognise the skills needed to tackle these;
- train and retrain for the required skills development.

The problems include recognising, accepting and working realistically to reduce the vulnerability of quality initiatives. In the following extract from a report from Birmingham, Whale gives a vivid impression of the problem and how it was tackled:

> There is a widespread view among headteachers in the city that Birmingham has been 'bedevilled' by initiatives – that, historically, successive initiatives have been conceived, have flourished and then died, leaving behind a legacy of resentment, cynicism and frustration. This had to be brought into the open and confronted. At every stage it has made us take great care about making promises that might not be sustainable, particularly in relation to resourcing and support.
>
> (Whale 1992: 201)

The disastrous consequences of over-organising educational initiatives have been highlighted by Newsam:

> It is unwise to predict the future, I know, but if I had to pick a candidate for future derision it would probably be the excessive detail in which [initiatives have been handed down] from formula funding to the National Curriculum itself and its testing procedures, so much is now being laid down by regulation. It is in this way that exciting ideas of which there have been a number in recent years are driven into bureaucratic sand.
>
> (Newsam 1992: 260)

The headteacher of the primary school which achieved BSI 5750 recognition pointed out this important precondition for the success of the lengthy and detailed work by the staff:

[In 1987] the school was one of twelve in Dudley which took part in the Getting Results and Solving Problems (GRASP) project, designed to assess and improve the achievement of schools. GRASP had led us to a collegiate management system where staff were used to discussing things freely . . . . It would be difficult to put BS 5750 into a school where the staff were not used to operating in an open climate.

(Merrick 1993: 5-6)

This is a good example of what has been argued strongly throughout this book. The school is the most significant arena for professional training and development when it provides what the teacher–researcher in School B in the previous chapter called 'a sharing–learning culture'. Middle managers are well placed to influence and strengthen this culture by using and sharing with their colleagues all the management skills presented and discussed in this book.

An inventory for the identification of roles and skills in teamwork

Directions: For each section distribute a total of ten points among the sentences which you think best describe your behaviour. These points may be distributed among several sentences: in extreme cases they might be spread among all the sentences or ten points may be given to a single sentence. Enter the points in the points table after Section 7.

1 What I believe I can contribute to a team:

(a) I think I can quickly see and take advantage of new opportunities.
(b) I can work well with a very wide range of people.
(c) Producing ideas is one of my natural assets.
(d) My ability rests in being able to draw people out whenever I detect they have something of value to contribute to group objectives.
(e) My capacity to follow through has much to do with my personal effectiveness.
(f) I am ready to face temporary unpopularity if it leads to worthwhile results in the end.
(g) I can usually sense what is realistic and likely to work.
(h) I can offer a reasoned case for alternative courses of action without introducing bias or prejudice.

2 If I have a possible shortcoming in teamwork it could be that:

(a) I am not at ease unless meetings are well structured and controlled and generally well conducted.
(b) I am inclined to be too generous towards others who have a valid viewpoint that has not been given a proper airing.
(c) I have a tendency to talk too much once the group gets on to new ideas.
(d) My objective outlook makes it difficult for me to join in readily and enthusiastically with colleagues.
(e) I am sometimes seen as forceful and authoritarian if there is a need to get something done.

(f) I find it difficult to lead from the front, perhaps because I am over-responsive to group atmosphere.
(g) I am apt to get too caught up in ideas that occur to me and so lose track of what is happening.
(h) My colleagues tend to see me as worrying over detail and the possibility that things may go wrong.

3 When involved in a project with other people:

(a) I have an aptitude for influencing people without pressuring them.
(b) My general vigilance prevents careless mistakes and omissions being made.
(c) I am ready to press for action to make sure that the meeting does not waste time or lose sight of the main objective.
(d) I can be counted on to contribute something original.
(e) I am always ready to back a good suggestion in the common interest.
(f) I am keen to look for the latest in new ideas and developments.
(g) I believe my capacity for judgement can help to bring about the right decisions.
(h) I can be relied upon to see that all essential work is organised.

4 My characteristic approach to group work is that:

(a) I have a quiet interest in getting to know colleagues better.
(b) I am not reluctant to challenge the views of others or to hold a minority view myself.
(c) I can usually find a line of argument to refute unsound propositions.
(d) I think I have a talent for making things work once a plan has to be put into operation.
(e) I have a tendency to avoid the obvious and to come out with the unexpected.
(f) I bring a touch of perfectionism to any job I undertake.
(g) I am ready to make use of contacts outside the group itself.
(h) While I am interested in all views I have no hesitation in making up my mind once a decision has to be made.

5 I gain satisfaction in a job because:

(a) I enjoy analysing situations and weighing up all the possible choices.
(b) I am interested in finding practical solutions to problems.
(c) I like to feel I am fostering good working relationships.
(d) I can have a strong influence on decisions.
(e) I can meet people who may have something new to offer.
(f) I can get people to agree on a necessary course of action.

(g) I feel in my element when I can give a task my full attention.

(h) I like to find a field that stretches my imagination.

6   If I am suddenly given a difficult task with limited time and unfamiliar people:

(a) I would feel like retiring to a corner to devise a way out of the impasse before developing a line.

(b) I would be ready to work with the person who showed the most positive approach.

(c) I would find some way of reducing the size of the task by establishing what different individuals might best contribute.

(d) My natural sense of urgency would help to ensure that we did not fall behind schedule.

(e) I believe I would keep cool and maintain my capacity to think straight.

(f) I would retain a steadiness of purpose in spite of the pressures.

(g) I would be prepared to take a positive lead if I felt the group was making no progress.

(h) I would open up discussions with a view to stimulating new thoughts and getting something moving.

7   With reference to the problems to which I am subject when working in groups:

(a) I am apt to show my impatience with those who are obstructing progress.

(b) Others may criticise me for being too analytical and insufficiently intuitive.

(c) My desire to ensure that work is done properly can hold up proceedings.

(d) I get bored rather easily and rely on one or two stimulating members to spark me off.

(e) I find it difficult to get started unless the goals are clear.

(f) I am sometimes poor at explaining and clarifying complex points that occur to me.

(g) I am conscious of demanding from others the things I cannot do myself.

(h) I hesitate to get my points across when I run up against real opposition.

Points table

Section	Item (a)	Item (b)	Item (c)	Item (d)	Item (e)	Item (f)	Item (g)	Item (h)
1								
2								
3								
4								
5								
6								
7								

Analysis sheet

Transpose the scores taken from the points table. Enter them section by section in the table below. Then add up the points in each column. The total of sub-totals should be 70.

Section	CW	CH	SH	IN	RI	ME	TW	CF
1	g	d	f	c	a	h	b	e
2	a	b	e	g	c	d	f	h
3	h	a	c	d	f	g	e	b
4	d	h	b	e	g	c	a	f
5	b	f	d	h	e	a	c	g
6	f	c	g	a	h	e	b	d
7	e	g	a	f	d	b	h	c
Totals								

CW: Company worker   CH: Chairperson/coordinator
SH: Shaper   IN: Innovator
RI: Resource investigator   ME: Monitor/evaluator
TW: Team worker   CF: Completor/finisher

This inventory is taken from Belbin (1981) *Management Teams: Why They Succeed or Fail*, London: Heinemann; © Belbin (1981).

References

Adair, J. (1983) *Effective Leadership*, London: Pan.

Albrecht, K. (1992) 'No eulogies for TQM', *The Total Quality Management Magazine*, May: 8–9.

Alexander, R., Rose, J. and Whitehead, C. (1992) *Curriculum Organisation and Classroom Practice in Primary Schools. A Discussion Paper*, London: Department of Education and Science Information Branch.

Arkin, A. (1993) 'Quality strained through jargon', *Times Educational Supplement*, May: 4–5.

Belbin, M. (1981) *Management Teams: Why They Succeed or Fail*, London: Heinemann.

Berkshire Education Department (1991) *Developing Managers*, Reading: Berkshire LEA.

Blackburn, K. (1986) 'Teacher appraisal' in M. Marland (ed.) *School Management Skills*, London: Heinemann.

Blake, R. R. and Mouton, J. S. (1985) *The Management Grid III*, Houston: Gulf Publishing Company.

Blanchard, K., Carew, D. and Parisi-Carew, E. (1992) *The One Minute Manager Builds High Performing Teams*, London: Harper Collins.

Bolam, R., McMahon, A., Pockington, K. and Weindling, D. (1993) *Effective Management in Schools: A Report for the Department for Education via the School Management Task Force Professional Working Party*, London: HMSO.

Bolton Business Ventures Ltd (undated) *Induction Training for Employees in Small Businesses*, Bolton: Bolton Business Ventures Ltd.

Bowring-Carr, E. (1993) 'The use of interactive video for staff development' in H. Green (ed.) *The School Management Handbook*, London: Kogan Page.

Bradley, H., Bollington, R., Dadds, M., Hopkins, D., Howard, J., Southworth, G. and West, M. (1989) *Report of the Evaluation of the School Teacher Appraisal Pilot Study*, Cambridge: Cambridge Institute of Education.

Cotgrove, S., Dunham, J. and Vamplew, C. (1971) *The Nylon Spinners*, London: Allen and Unwin.

Courtis, J. (1988) *Interviews: Skills and Strategies*, London: Institute of Personnel Management.

Department of Education and Science (1985) *Better Schools*, London: HMSO.

Department of Education and Science (1991) 'Circular 7/91: Local Management of Schools: Further Guidance,' London: HMSO.

Duffy, M. (1990) 'Feedback benefits', *Times Educational Supplement*, May 25–37.

Dunham, J. (1965) 'Appropriate leadership patterns', *Educational Research* 7(2): 115–26.

Dunham, J. (1992) *Stress in Teaching*, 2nd edition, London: Routledge.

Edwards, G. (1993) 'Review of Southworth, G. (1990) staff selection in the primary school', Oxford: Blackwell in *Education Today* 43(1): 62.

Everard, K. B. and Morris, C. (1985) *Effective School Management*, London: Harper and Row.

Fiedler, F. E. and Chemers, M. M. (1984) *Improving Leadership Effectiveness: The Leader Match Concept*, New York: Wiley.

Finn, R. (1993) 'The effective route to school-based development' in H. Green (ed.) *The School Management Handbook*, London: Kogan Page.

Glatter, R. (1993) 'Opportunities for management development for teachers' in H. Green (ed.) *The School Management Handbook*, London: Kogan Page.

Gratus, J. (1988) *Successful Interviewing*, London: Penguin Business.

Grice, C. and Hanke, M. (1990) 'Suspending judgements: teacher appraisal', *Education Today* 40(2): 42–4.

Hancock, R. and Settle, D. (1992) *Teacher Appraisal and Self Evaluation: A Practical Guide*, Oxford: Blackwell.

Handy, C. (1988) 'Cultural forces in schools' in R. Glatter, C. Riches and M. Masterton (eds) *Understanding School Management*, Milton Keynes: The Open University Press.

Henley Distance Learning Ltd (1991) *The Task of Management*, Henley: Henley Distance Learning Ltd.

Herzberg, F. (1968) *Work and the Nature of Man*, New York: World.

Honey, P. and Mumford, A. (1989) 'Trials and tribulations', the *Guardian*, 19 December: 19–21.

Humphreys, P. T. (1983) 'Recruitment and selection' in D. Lock and N. Farrow (eds) *The Gower Book of Management*, Aldershot: Gower.

Jay, A. (1976) *How to Run a Meeting*, London: Video Arts.

Jenks, I. M. and Kelly, J. M. (1985) *Don't Do, Delegate*, London: Kogan Page.

Kehoe, L. (1993) 'That vision thing again', *The Financial Times*, 10 August: 7.

McMahon, A. and Bolam, R. (1990) *Management Development and Educational Reform: A Handbook for Primary Schools*, London: Paul Chapman Publishing.

Marland, M. (ed.) (1986) *School Management Skills*, London: Heinemann.

Maslow, A. H. (1943), 'A theory of human motivation' in V. H. Vroom and E. L. Deci (eds) (1992) *Management and Motivation*, 2nd edition, London: Penguin.

Merrick, N. (1993) 'Prototype for progress', *Times Educational Supplement*, May: 5.

Millar, R., Crute, V. and Hargie, O. (1992) *Professional Interviewing*, London: Routledge.

Morris, M. (1993) 'Catalogue of woe', *Education*, 16 July: 79.

Murgatroyd, S. (1992) 'A new frame for managing schools: total quality management (TQM), *School Organisation* 12(2): 175–201.

Newsam, Sir P. (1992) 'Educational reform: the past has lessons to teach the future' in T. Simkins, L. Ellison and V. Garrett (eds) *Implementing Educational Reform: The Early Lessons*, Harlow: Longman.

Oldroyd, D., Smith, K. and Lee, J. (1984) *School Based Staff Development Activities*, London: Longman.

Peters, T. (1988) *Thriving on Chaos*, London: Macmillan.

Plant, T. (1987) *Managing Change and Making It Stick*, London: Fontana/Collins.

Poster, C. and Poster, D. (1993) *Teacher Appraisal: A Guide to Training*, 2nd edition, London: Routledge.

Prior, P. (1977) *Leadership is not a Bowler Hat*, Newton Abbott: David & Charles.

Robson, M. (1984) *Quality Circles in Action*, Aldershot: Gower.

School Teachers' Review Body Report (1993) *Times Educational Supplement*, 26 March: 6.

Shropshire Education Department (1993) *Management Development in Primary Schools*, Shrewsbury: Shropshire Education Department.

Simpkins, T., Ellison, L. and Garrett, V. (eds) (1992) *Implementing Educational Reform: The Early Lessons*, Harlow: Longman.

Singer, E. J. (1979) *Effective Management Coaching*, 2nd edition, London: Institute of Personnel Management.

Tannenbaum, R. and Schmidt, W. H. (1973) 'How to choose a leadership pattern', *Harvard Business Review*, May–June: 162–79.

Thompson, P. (1987) *School Self-Evaluation*, Scarborough: Teachers' Publishing Group.

Threlfall, B. (1991) *Your Approach to Interview Questions*, London: New Education Press.

Travers, C. and Cooper, C. (1990) *Survey of Occupational Stress Among Teachers in the United Kingdom*, Manchester: University of Manchester Institute of Science and Technology.

Warrington, M. (1993) 'Non-teaching support staff' in H. Green (ed.) *The School Management Handbook*, 2nd edition, London: Kogan Page.

Warwick, D. (1983) *Staff Appraisal*, London: The Industrial Society Press.

Waters, D. (1991) 'Ten Commandments for more effective meetings', *Primary World* 1(2).

Whale, E. (1992) 'Quality development in Birmingham' in T. Simkins, L. Ellison and V. Garrett (eds) *Implementing Educational Reform: The Early Lessons*, Harlow: Longman.

Whitfield, M. (1992) 'Performance gets a hand', *The Independent on Sunday*, 19 April: 31.

Wood, I. (1993) *Your Middle Management Role*, London: New Education Press.

Woodcock, M. (1979) *Team Development Manual*, Aldershot: Gower.

Wortley, B. (1993) 'The role of subject coordinators in primary schools: the state of the art', *Education Today* 43(1): 43–7.

Wragg, T. (1993) 'Kill or be killed, if we let the free market rule our lives', *Observer*, 12 September: 57.

Index

short-term 48; supply 48, 90; *see
also* selection
teaching styles 147
team: benefits of teamwork 46–50,
145; building 50–2; chairing
meetings 2, 55–8, 70, 119, 143; and
change management 116;
management 33, 42–3, 53–5; role
inventory 53–5, 151–4; and stress
management 138, 140; and task
culture 44–5
Thompson, Peter 101–2
threat: as opportunity 122–5;
reviewing 76–7
Three Circle Model 32–4
Threlfall, B. 88
time: non-contact 1–2, 130, 142;
pressures xiii, 4, 111–13
time management 106, 109–14;
contract 110–14; organisational
114; theft 109–10
total quality management (TQM)
147–9
training 103–8; and appraisal 98–9,
103; and change management 124;
distance learning 106; identifying
needs 6–8, 53, 66–8, 69, 71, 73,

76–7, 88, 94; and interactive videos
106–7; lack of 2–6; need for 1–2,
103–8, 142, 145; school-based 107;
and staff selection 81; and stress
management 138–9
Travers, C. 130
truancy, recording 2–3
Two Factor Theory of motivation
38–41

values, management 42, 122
Vamplew, C. 39
video, interactive 106–7
vision, developing 120, 121

Warrington, Michael 112, 141
Warwick, D. 99
Waters, D. 57–8
weaknesses: and appraisal 102, 103;
reviewing 66, 67, 76–7; in
teamwork 53–5
Whale, E. 149
Whitehead, C. 6
Whitfield, M. 95
Woodcock, M. 51
Wortley, B. 5–6
Wragg, T. 122